READING IN THE CONTENT AREAS
SCIENCE 2

Laura Stark Johnson

PERMISSIONS

HARRY N. ABRAMS, INC. for "Water—the Essence of Life" and "If the Oceans Should Die." Reprinted from The Ocean World of Jacques Cousteau—Oasis in Space. By Jacques Cousteau. Published in 1977 by The World Book Publishing Co. c/o Harry N. Abrams, Inc. New York. All rights reserved.

CHICAGO TRIBUNE for "Wonderworker." © Copyrighted, Chicago Tribune Company, all rights reserved, used with permission.

ENSLOW PUBLISHERS, INC., for "Genetic Challenge" from *Genes, Medicine, and You* by Alvin and Virginia Silverstein, Enslow Publishers, Inc., © 1989.

FRANKLIN WATTS, INC. for "Science Ethics." From *Science Ethics.* Copyright © 1985 by David Newton. Reprinted with permission of the publisher, Franklin Watts, Inc.

GROLIER, INC., for "Chemical Reactions." Reprinted with permission of *The New Book of Popular Science,* copyright 1988, Grolier, Inc.

MACMILLAN PUBLISHING COMPANY for "What Makes Things Move?" Reprinted with permission of Atheneum Publishers, an imprint of Macmillan Publishing Company from *Secrets of the Universe* by Paul Fleisher. Illustrated by Patricia Keeler. Text copyright © 1987 Paul Fleisher. Illustrations copyright © 1987 Patricia A. Keeler.

for "A Moving Frontier." Reprinted with permission of Macmillan Publishing Company from *The Wonders of Science* by Irving Adler. Copyright © 1966.

MCINTOSH AND OTIS, INC., for "The Miracle of Vitamins." Copyright © 1964 by Doris Faber. Reprinted by permission of McIntosh and Otis, Inc.

for "The Time of Your Life." Copyright © 1968 by Shirley Moore. Reprinted by permission of McIntosh and Otis, Inc.

NATIONAL GEOGRAPHIC SOCIETY for "Tomorrow's Transportation." Reprinted by permission, National Geographic Books for World Explorers. Copyright © 1985 National Geographic Society.

NATIONAL OCEANIC AND ATMOSPHERIC ADMINISTRATION for "The Sea" from *Our Living Ocean.*

NEWSWEEK, INC., for "This Is Big. Reeeeally Big." from *Newsweek,* June 4, 1990, © 1990, Newsweek, Inc. All rights reserved. Reprinted by permission.

for "An Icy Warning of a Global Warming" from *Newsweek,* December 28, 1987, © 1987, Newsweek, Inc. All rights reserved. Reprinted by permission.

RANDOM HOUSE, INC., for "What Fire Is." From *All About Fire* by Raymond Holden, illustrated by Clifford Stead, Jr. Copyright © 1964 by Raymond Holden. Reprinted by permission of Random House, Inc.

SCHOLASTIC INC. for "All that Glitters, Spreads, Stretches, and Conducts" from *Science World,* March 1989. Copyright © 1989 by Scholastic Inc. Reprinted by permission.

PATRICIA SKALKA for "It's Not the Heat, It's the Humidity." Reprinted with permission from the July 1989 *Reader's Digest.*

ROBERT SPEER for "Snow in Every Shape and Form," as reprinted in the *Chicago Tribune,* December 25, 1987.

TIME INC. for "The New Zoo: A Modern Ark." Copyright 1978 The Time Inc. Magazine Company. Reprinted by permission.

NOEL VIETMEYER for "Who Needs Spiders." Reprinted with permission from the June 1989 *Reader's Digest.*

WORLD BOOK, INC. for "What Makes Paint Stick." From *Science Year, The 1989 World Book Annual Science Supplement.* © 1988 World Book, Inc. By permission of the publisher.

ISBN 0-88336-124-8

Copyright © 1992
New Readers Press
Publishing Division of Laubach Literacy International
Box 131, Syracuse, New York 13210-0131

Printed in the United States of America

Sponsoring Editor: Christina M. Jagger
Project Editor: Heidi Stephens
Cover Design: Patricia Rapple
Cover Art: Stephen Rhodes

9 8 7 6 5 4 3 2

Table of Contents

What kinds of things might you consider when deciding what is the right or wrong action to take in a certain situation? Ethics are beliefs and rules about right and wrong. Read the following selection to learn about some of the ethical issues that scientists face.

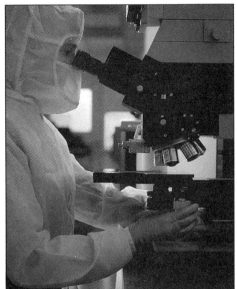

Science Ethics

Most societies and most social institutions have certain *ethical standards*. For example, premeditated murder is usually considered to be wrong in most societies. Societies generally do not allow individuals to argue that they have an ethical right to take someone else's life simply because that action will be to their own personal, social, economic, or emotional benefit.

In many cases, society's ethical rules—written or unwritten—can be a powerful influence on our ultimate decisions about right and wrong. We may be able to think of many personal reasons for following a

A scientist records observations in an experiment with mice.

particular course of action. But we may also know that friends, business colleagues, and society at large think that that choice is wrong. The force of this social pressure, then, can override any and all personal factors involved in our decision.

The Game of Science

Ethics means "playing by the rules of the game." We can learn about ethical issues in science by understanding some of the rules by which "the game of science" is played.

The *purpose* of the game of science is fairly simple: to make true statements about the natural world. These statements can be as simple as "The melting point of ice is 0° C," or as comprehensive as "All objects in the universe feel an attraction to one another."

The primary *method* by which these statements develop is observation. Some scientists observe nature directly. Astronomers, for example, learn about stars by studying them through telescopes. But most scientists study nature through experiments, specially designed situations which allow them to study one specific part of nature at a time. Scientists report the results of their observations and experiments in written reports, articles in professional journals, speeches at conventions, and informal conversation at other scientific meetings.

Probably the most important rule of the game of science tells when we know a statement is *true* in science. After all, anyone can look through a telescope or do an experiment and write down some observations. But how do we know those observations are true?

The answer is by *confirmation*. Once scientist A writes down a result, other scientists will begin to use that result in their own work. As they use the new idea, they'll find out whether or not the idea "works." If it does work time after time, the new idea is confirmed and becomes part of scientific truth. If the idea does not work for other scientists the way it did for scientist A, the original research has to be repeated and checked until an error is found.

Some people say that science is "self-correcting" because errors will always be found out. Suppose a scientist makes up the result of an experiment. Other scientists who try to use those results will discover that they are false. Errors and dishonest reports cannot, therefore, survive for long in science. At least, that's what the rules of science predict. This, however, may not always be the case.

Deciding on Right and Wrong in Science

Ethical problems have concerned men and women almost from the moment humans first began studying the natural world in a systematic way. The ethical code[1] which doctors recite when they join the medical profession today goes back at least 2,000 years. The Hippocratic oath defines what ethical behavior is when a physician works with his or her patients. The oath describes not only the methods that doctors should and should not use in treating the ill, but also the code of conduct they should follow in working with patients. One part of the code says, for example, "Whatever, in connection with my professional practice, or not in connection with it, I see or hear, in the life of men, which ought not to be spoken of abroad, I will not divulge[2] as reckoning that all such should be kept secret."

---

1. **code:** set of rules
2. **divulge:** tell about; reveal

Swedish inventor Alfred Nobel, who lived from 1833–1896

Perhaps the most famous historical example of an ethical dilemma[3] in science comes from the life of the Swedish inventor Alfred Nobel. In 1866, Nobel discovered the explosive called dynamite. The discovery of dynamite made Nobel's fortune. He died in 1896, a multimillionaire ... but also a troubled man.

Nobel realized the terrible weapon of war he had given the world. At one time, he thought that the use of dynamite in battle would produce so much devastation that the nations of the world would begin to find ways other than war to settle their differences. "Perhaps," he wrote, "my [dynamite] factories will end war sooner than your [peace] congresses. On the day when two army corps will be able to annihilate[4] each other in one second, all civilized nations will recoil from war in horror and disband their forces."

In the years following his discovery of dynamite, Nobel was constantly troubled by the ethical implications of what he had done. In the end, was his discovery a "good" or "bad" thing for human civilization? Was the positive benefit of having a powerful new construction tool greater than the negative risk of greater pain and suffering from the use of dynamite in warfare?

Of course, each person would answer that question in his or her own way. Part of Nobel's answer was to leave his entire fortune, some $8 million, to the betterment of human society. In his will, he established a trust fund with this money from which to award prizes in literature, the sciences, and the pursuit of peace. These Nobel Prizes were one man's way of resolving the ethical questions raised by his accomplishments in science.

---

3. dilemma: difficult choice
4. annihilate: wipe out; destroy completely

Ethical Issues in Science Today

Even though scientists overall have no *formal* code of ethics, they do have an informal understanding about the right way to do research. (Some scientific societies *do* have formal codes, however.) The scientific community has, over many years, come to agree upon certain ethically acceptable procedures for doing and reporting on research.

Still, ethical issues in science are seldom clear-cut, black-and-white issues. Even though a scientist may know what colleagues think is the right way to do things, he or she may choose to do something else. Other factors may make, for this individual scientist, this choice the ethically correct one.

For example, suppose that a scientist is eager to work on an important military project for the government because he or she believes it will greatly strengthen the nation's defensive position. Taking part in the project is, for this scientist, an act of patriotism.

But one condition of working on the project might be that the scientist cannot communicate research results to other scientists: the project is classified as "top secret." This would be a violation of one part of the scientific community's informal code of ethics that says that all research results must always be shared with all other members of the scientific community. In this case, certain considerations (national security) may convince a scientist to act in a way (suppressing information) that other scientists might normally think of as unethical.

Ethical dilemmas such as this one have become more important for scientists in recent years because of the vastly expanded role of science in our everyday lives. Today, scientists have to think not just about the way their actions will affect the scientific community, but what impact they will have on the community at large.

The case of the military researcher illustrates this point. He or she may decide to ignore one of the ethical tenets[5] of science because social, economic, political, or other factors seem more important in this particular case.

Thus, we see today an increasing number of people, both inside and outside the scientific community, having to think about ethical implications of scientific research. Consider just a few of the issues about which you may have heard or read:

---

5. tenets: principles; beliefs

- If scientists are able to make larger and more powerful nuclear weapons, should they continue to do so, without limit?
- If scientists learn how to control the expression of genetic characteristics (genetic disease, hair color, intelligence, etc.), is there any point at which they should go no further with such research?
- What obligations do scientists have to report on incomplete, incorrect, or fraudulent research done by their colleagues?
- Do scientists have the right to spend public tax dollars on "pure" research, such as research on planets or in outer space, that seems to have no promise of improving life on earth?

Scientists are not always eager to take part in this debate on ethics. Most have been trained to believe that science operates according to a rather strict set of rules that govern their research. When those rules conflict with social, political, economic, legal, religious, and moral factors, they would prefer to let other members of society work out the conflict.

But ignoring their part in this debate has become more and more difficult for scientists. In some cases, like that of the scientist faced with a decision about participating in military research, the issue just *can't* be ignored. In other cases, scientists are simply beginning to see that they have an ethical responsibility to help resolve issues. For one thing, the kinds of research that scientists choose to do and the kinds of discoveries they make often determine the social and political issues of the next decade.

Also, scientists simply have too much technical knowledge in the field to leave these decisions entirely to politicians, religious leaders, sociologists, and other citizens. Understanding and solving modern social, political, and economic issues requires, therefore, the active participation of scientists.

In still other cases, nonscientists are *forcing* scientists to become involved in ethical debates. Some nonscientists have, for example, challenged certain types of research projects in the courts—and won! When this happens, scientists have no choice but to pay more attention to the social and ethical implications of their work.

From *Science Ethics,* by David E. Newton

Unit 1: Biology

the science that deals with the study of living things

COMPOSITION WITH THREE FIGURES FRAGMENT, 1932, Fernand Leger, oil on canvas. The Carnegie Museum of Art, Pittsburgh; Gift of Mr. and Mrs. Henry J. Heinz, II, 54.19

What substances do you think scientists study to find materials for new medicines? Would you be surprised to learn that scientists often look in dirt? Read this selection to learn about a determined scientist whose valuable discovery had just such a beginning.

Wonderworker

Last year in the United States about 1,500 human hearts were lifted from the chests of clinically dead people and stitched into the chests of transplant recipients. About 1,100 patients received donor livers after complex operations. An additional 9,000 kidneys ended up in abdomens that nature had never meant for them.

The grafted organs, sparked by new nerve connections, immediately set up shop in their new homes. Hearts began beating; livers broke down chemicals into disposable products; kidneys filtered wastes and flushed them away by the gallons—all working steadily to restore health.

Almost simultaneously and with equal determination, the bodies started to reject the good samaritans.

Even as a surgeon had completed a lifesaving transplant procedure, microscopic pieces of the new organ invariably floated off in the bloodstream, perhaps to a neighborhood lymph node[1] where the standing army of white blood cells known as T cells—one group of the body's infection-fighting agents—spotted the pieces as foreign and began producing antibodies[2] to kill them.

Other circulating T cells, prowling relentlessly throughout the body in search of alien bacteria, stumbled over the new graft itself. These lymphocytes[3] blindly blazed into action, secreting potent substances with odd-sounding

---

1. **lymph node:** a mass of tissue that is part of one of the body's systems for fighting infection
2. **antibodies:** substances that destroy or weaken bacteria or poisons
3. **lymphocytes:** white blood cells, such as T cells, that are produced in the lymph nodes and help fight infection

names—migration inhibitory factor, interleukin 2, gamma interferon—that activated more defenders to swarm over the new graft and kill it.

Because nature never had envisioned an era when vital organs would be routinely transferred from person to person, the body in such a situation mindlessly takes the side of certain death over life. A kidney will shut down; a liver stops working, causing the brain to lapse into coma; a heart struggles, then ceases beating. Unless something is done, the new organs have no chance at all.

Except for cyclosporine.

Without the miraculous drug, an estimated 150,000 transplant patients worldwide wouldn't be living today. They wouldn't be walking around with someone else's heart, lung, liver, kidney, pancreas, skin, intestine, or bone marrow in their bodies.

These lucky survivors may not know of Swiss immunologist Jean-François Borel, the discoverer of cyclosporine, but each morning they toast him. They mix their bitter, oily cyclosporine solution with something like orange juice or chocolate milk, and the miracle molecule stops their immune systems from rejecting the foreign body part. It lets them get on with their lives.

"Cyclosporine comes from a fungus,[4] basically, and is found in dirt," Borel said in a recent interview in Chicago. The modest, soft-spoken scientist who describes himself as "only a mouse doctor" had come to the city to receive the "Gift of Life" award from the National Kidney Foundation of Illinois.

"You can scratch the earth's surface, and the fungus that produces cyclosporine is down about an inch deep in the soil," he explained. "It may be found anywhere; these fungi are widespread all over the world."

Yet no other drug has proved so Olympian in its power to challenge perhaps the most fundamental biological system in nature: the body's determination to reject unwanted intruders.

However, even today, years after a vacationing employee of the Basel-based pharmaceutical house Sandoz Ltd. serendipitously picked up the mystery microbe[5] in a handful of Norwegian soil above the Arctic circle, no one knows for sure how cyclosporine works.

Not even Borel, 55, now senior scientist in immunology at Sandoz, who at the time was a staff researcher investigating new pharmaceuticals. As a Sandoz employee, Borel has made no money for his discovery. Yet without his fierce determination, the drug would have been doomed to oblivion.[6]

Drug companies sample dirt constantly, Borel said. "We look for microorganisms because they produce metabolites, interesting compounds that sometimes are chemically novel.[7] Our lab screens as many as 30,000 such compounds a year."

Placed in petri dishes,[8] the visiting microbes are fed a nourishing broth

---

4. **fungus:** type of organism, examples of which are molds, mildews, mushrooms, rusts, and toadstools
5. **microbe:** a tiny living thing that can be seen only with a microscope
6. **oblivion:** state of being forgotten
7. **novel:** new and not the same as anything known
8. **petri dishes:** shallow, circular glass dishes with loose covers used in science labs

of agar, a "chicken soup" for cells. Soon various fungi and molds obligingly appear. The educated eyes of microbiologists study them carefully, looking for something new.

Nobody looks with more eagerness than Borel. But so far, he has seen nothing as remarkable as cyclosporine. An astounding number of research papers have been written about the drug. But they deal mostly with proper management of patients and possible new uses for cyclosporine, not with the mysteries of how it happened to be.

Despite the laboratory wizardry that brought the synthetic sulfa drugs to humanity, the world's most interesting pharmaceuticals still come from living creatures: sponges, periwinkles, fungi, bacteria.

The white fungus *Tolypocladium inflatum* makes cyclosporine.

"It looked like just a white mold," Borel recalled. "But it was a new type of white mold. When it was found in 1972, I knew right away it was something special. The drug later gave us a lot of trouble, and many people thought I was a fool for sticking with it."

At first the Sandoz company had hoped the new compound would prove to be an antibiotic,[9] Borel said. "We tested for that."

The test was straightforward. Scientists infected mice with a germ and gave them the new compound to see if it could cure them. The Sandoz mice merely dropped dead. Cyclosporine, it turned out, was helpless against germs.

"But we noticed something important," Borel said. "The drug was not toxic. The animals tolerated it well. Some microorganisms make compounds that are terribly toxic. We just throw them away. A rule of thumb is that the activity of a drug equals its toxicity—the more potent a drug, the more poisonous. But this wasn't the case with cyclosporine."

The benign[10] nature of the chemically interesting cyclosporine intrigued Borel, even after it had flopped as an antibiotic and his bosses had told him nothing good would come of it.

"They ordered me to pour cyclosporine down the drain," Borel recalled, grinning slyly. "Several times I was forbidden to work with it. So I worked in secret."

Indeed Borel later was to risk his life, not to mention his career, for this mysterious "fungal metabolite," as he calls it, that utterly transformed transplant surgery.

But what could the fungus do? Could it be a heart drug? a cancer drug? In the course of experimenting, Borel injected cyclosporine into a culture of white blood cells. Remarkably the fungus blocked the ability of the immune cells to grow or function. But they didn't die. Unlike other immunosuppressive drugs,[11] cyclosporine didn't kill lymphocytes. It merely muzzled them.

"At the time, rejection was treated with anticancer drugs that killed all rapidly dividing cells," Borel said. "Tumor cells grow very fast, but so do

---

9. **antibiotic:** substance that stops the growth of or kills certain microorganisms
10. **benign:** not threatening to health or life
11. **immunosuppressive drugs:** medicines that keep the immune system from doing its job, which is to attack foreign matter in the body

the cells that the body summons up to respond to an infection or an alien organ. That's why anticancer drugs were used."

But such drugs don't care what cells they kill. They smash into cells like buckshot, destroying blood cells, hair follicles, and cells of the stomach lining, as well as cancer.

"You get diarrhea and anemia, or low blood counts. You get nausea," Borel said. "These are good drugs. But they can cause tremendous side effects."

Still, he adds, there wasn't much commercial incentive for a drug firm to develop a new immunosuppressant. Transplantation had ground to a halt in the early 1970s. The average one-year survival rate for a transplanted kidney in the United States was only 50 percent; for bone marrow transplants, between 20 and 50 percent. Heart transplantation had been virtually abandoned.

"Immunology, my field, was bursting with new discoveries," Borel said, "but unfortunately there was nothing for the doctor to use to help patients. This is why I believed so much in this drug. I thought it could have a big effect: that it might even save the idea of organ transplantation, make its practice broaden, and give people a chance to stay alive.

"So I found myself assuming the role of a product champion, not just a scientist. I was pushing the drug against the will of company management."

Jean-François Borel (right) receives the 1988 "Gift of Life" award from the National Kidney Foundation of Illinois. The presenter is Harold D. Schwartz, who received the previous year's award.

Quietly testing the drug in animals that had undergone organ transplants, Borel obtained stunning results. Cyclosporine worked entirely differently from other antirejection drugs.

"It doesn't go after rapidly dividing cells but only the very specific kind of white blood cell [T cells] responsible for the immune defense response," Borel said.

By 1977, however, Borel had a problem. The drug didn't seem to be water-soluble.[12] "Unless injected directly into the blood, it just went through an animal's body. Of course, that would never work for patients. I wanted them to be able to swallow it."

This problem nearly cost society cyclosporine. Once the company accepted his work, their researchers

---

12. **water-soluble:** able to be dissolved in water

found that when cyclosporine was given in the form of a gelatin capsule, it was not absorbed in the bloodstream of healthy volunteers, including Borel himself. Maybe the drug worked only in animals but not in humans? Once again Borel was told to shelve cyclosporine.

The pressures on him, he said, were "tremendous. But I knew from my animals that depending on the solution you put it into you could dramatically increase the absorption rate."

Again, Borel was virtually a lone voice. He proposed that if cyclosporine were mixed as a kind of cocktail with water, alcohol, and a solvent,[13] it would be absorbed by the human body. Other scientists argued that Borel was wrong this time. He had done his best. Let it go.

He demanded that they let him drink such a concoction.

"I told them, 'Look, let me try it myself. I want to prove to you that it can be done, that the body will absorb it.'

"The conditions were very controlled. People prepared the substance the way I wanted. Then I drank it, with them all huddled around me. I took samples of my blood several times. They measured how much of it had gotten in."

By experimenting on himself before cyclosporine's toxicity was known, Borel joined the ranks of the most storied medical researchers: he went first and saved one of the most fantastic drugs of all time.

"Oh, it didn't hurt me," he stressed. "I got a little high, that was all. But I proved my point—the drug got into my blood."

In 1983, after tests with more than 2,000 kidney and heart transplant patients, cyclosporine was approved by the Food and Drug Administration.

Transplanted kidneys, which had only a 50 percent chance of surviving the first year with conventional immunosuppressive therapy, now have a better than 90 percent chance with cyclosporine. The success rate for hearts jumped from virtually nil to more than 80 percent. Livers doubled from 35 to 70 percent.

Borel's dream is to develop drugs with specific organ tolerance. "By that, I mean you'd give a patient a kidney and a drug that saves that kidney but leaves the rest of the immune system free to fight infection. That way, we probably could stop all medication after a period.

"Cyclosporine certainly can't do that yet," Borel said.

But maybe there's some other mold out there in the dirt somewhere that can.

"Cyclosporine probably was the drug of a lifetime for me," Borel concluded with a sigh. "But every day when I go into work, I'm still looking for something better."

---

13. **solvent:** a substance that can dissolve other substances

---

"Wonderworker," by Peter Gorner, from the *Chicago Tribune*

How can what you eat affect your health? More than 200 years ago, a ship's doctor designed an experiment to find out why crews of sailors got deathly ill on long trips. Read to find out how this doctor's study helped lay the groundwork for a whole branch of science—nutrition.

Back in the year 1747, a British warship put out to sea on a routine mission. Its task was to patrol the waters off the southern coast of England, lest by some chance an unfriendly vessel be approaching shore. Not once did the officers and men aboard the *Salisbury* find a sign of any suspicious foreign frigate during their whole three months afloat—and yet this seemingly uneventful voyage is still remembered.

It is remembered more than 200 years later because an enemy did attack the *Salisbury* and was defeated. The sailors on the British man-of-war never saw the black smoke of this foe's guns, for the enemy that struck was of an entirely different and deadlier sort than any mere opposing ship. This enemy, which killed more seamen in those days than guns and storms put together, was the mysterious and fearful disease known as scurvy. To fight this dread scourge, the 60 cannon mounted on the oaken decks of the *Salisbury* were useless. But by a flash of genius one man in the ship's crew was able, on that otherwise routine cruise, to show the world the way to conquer scurvy.

He was James Lind, a thoughtful young Scotsman serving as the ship's medical officer. What Dr. Lind accomplished on board the

Salisbury earned him and his ship a secure place in history, for the conquest of scurvy ranks as one of the major medical victories of all time. But only in the past half a century has the deeper significance of Dr. Lind's achievement been understood—and now he is honored even more than he was by the scientists closer to his own era. He is recognized as the first important figure in a whole branch of science unknown in his own day—the science we call nutrition, which is the study of the food we eat and how it is used by our bodies. In fact, before the exciting discoveries of modern nutritionists can be described, it is necessary to go back two centuries to start with the story of Dr. Lind.

Only a few weeks after he set sail on the *Salisbury,* the 31-year-old physician spotted the first signs of scurvy. Several men in the crew complained of feeling too weak to clamber up the masts to rig the sails—and clearly they were not putting on any pretense from laziness. Their eyes looked sunken, their gums bled often, and ugly sores erupted all over their skin. With the certainty born of hard experience, Dr. Lind knew that unless some miracle intervened, the men would grow steadily weaker and very likely die in anguish.

A great reader, Dr. Lind had already spent hour after hour picking out references to scurvy in old manuscripts. He knew that the disease had afflicted people throughout recorded history, on land as well as at sea. In dusty tomes, he had noted report after report about outbreaks of scurvy in towns under siege, when fresh food became scarce—and even in the Bible he had found a case he diagnosed[1] as scurvy. This, he felt sure, had been the malady that afflicted Job after the loss of all his flocks and his grain, when Job said: "By the great force of my disease is my skin changed; it bindeth me about as the collar of my coat … my skin is black upon me and my bones are burned with heat."

---

1. diagnosed: identified a condition by observing its signs

From all of his reading, however, as well as from his own experience, Dr. Lind well knew that scurvy struck more often at sea than on land—and he thought he knew why. It seemed obvious to him that the disease was in some way related to the kind of food available, and aboard ship the diet of the ordinary seamen hardly surpassed famine fare on dry land. While awaiting favorable winds, sailors in those days sometimes lived for weeks on salt meat the color and the texture of old leather, with only wormy dried biscuits and slimy water to make up the rest of their meal. Even under the best of conditions, an additional ration of rancid[2] cheese or butter, or perhaps a stew of dried beans, was about all the ordinary sailor could expect.

---

2. **rancid:** rotten; spoiled

The officers aboard ship had money to buy their own provisions, though, and even in this age before the advent of any sort of refrigeration they usually stocked barrels of decent meat, preserved in brine, as well as some vegetables and preserved fruits. And scurvy among officers was comparatively rare. Could their better diet be the reason? Dr. Lind thought it could at least partly explain why common sailors fell prey to scurvy so much more frequently than their officers.

With the instinct of a born scientist, Dr. Lind planned one of the most significant experiments in the whole history of medicine. The very heart of scientific research is the idea that any experiment must be controlled—that is, to make sure a particular method for accomplishing a desired end is really effective, it must be compared with other possible methods, under circumstances as nearly similar as it is feasible[3] to make them. Guided only by his own good judgment, Dr. Lind worked out a model controlled experiment.

"On the twentieth of May, 1747, I selected 12 patients in the scurvy on board the *Salisbury* at sea," he later wrote. "Their cases were as similar as I could have them. They all lay together in one place, being a proper apartment for the sick in the forehold; and had one diet common to all, viz. water gruel sweetened with sugar in the morning, fresh mutton broth oftentimes for dinner, at other times light pudding, boiled biscuit with sugar etc., and for supper barley with raisins, rice and currants, sage and wine or the like."

Dr. Lind's notebooks also held the hint of a more practical cure for scurvy accidentally discovered by the crew of a Dutch ship sailing home from Spain in 1564. Most of the seamen aboard the vessel had fallen dreadfully ill of the disease, but by a fortunate chance the main bulk of the ship's cargo consisted of Spanish oranges and lemons ordered by Dutch merchants. Some of the ailing seamen thought to suck the juice of the fruit—and their symptoms quickly disappeared.

From more recent sources, too, Dr. Lind had note after note saying that some fruit or fresh vegetable had stopped scurvy like magic. But was this magic? Or could such cures be counted on to take place whenever fresh food was eaten? With his dozen scurvy victims aboard the *Salisbury,* Dr. Lind set out to find the answer.

Put in scientific terms, he experimented with six different diet supplements: to his first group of two men, he gave a quart of apple cider

---

3. **feasible:** able to be done; possible

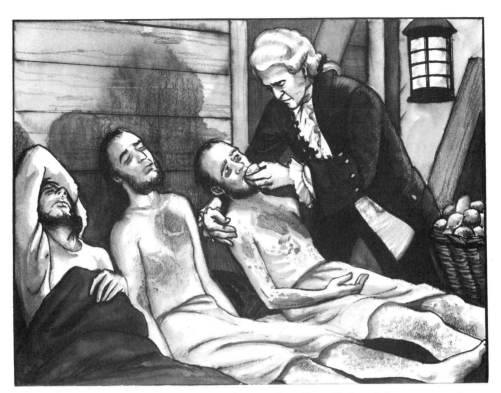

three times a day in addition to the regular diet all the sick men ate; the second group got two spoonfuls of vinegar thrice daily, and several drops of vinegar in their loblolly, which was what the sailors called the thin gruel that was the base of all the diets; another group got a medicine known as elixir vitriol, composed of diluted sulfuric acid and alcohol flavored with ginger and cinnamon; still another, a medicine made of garlic, mustard, and some ground-up herbs; and two other men, merely half a pint of salty sea water to wash down their meals. To the two lucky men in the sixth group, Dr. Lind gave two oranges and one lemon daily for six days, till his limited fruit supply ran out.

In his own words, this is what happened: "The consequence was, that the most sudden and visible good effects were perceived from the use of the oranges and lemons; one of those who had taken them being at the end of six days fit for duty. The spots were not at the same time quite off his body, nor his gums sound, but without any other medicine he became quite healthy before we came into Plymouth. The other was the best recovered of any in his condition, and being deemed pretty well, was appointed nurse to the rest of the sick."

"Some persons," Dr. Lind wrote a few years later, "cannot be brought to believe that a disease so fatal and so dreadful can be cured or prevented by such easy means. They would have more faith in an elaborate composition dignified with the title of 'an antiscorbutic golden elixir,' or the like." The "some persons" he meant were on the Board of the Care of Sick and Wounded Seamen of the British Admiralty, a group of hidebound[4] officers who—for many years—blindly refused to heed Dr. Lind.

In the British navy then, it was traditional to issue each seaman a drink of rum and water once every day. What Dr. Lind fervently urged was the addition of an ounce or two of concentrated lemon juice to this daily drink of grog—and he even experimented on shore with various ways of bottling the precious juice, so that a supply ample for a large crew on a long voyage could easily be stored afloat. But still the board resisted ordering juice for every man, and still the toll of sailors killed by scurvy continued to mount. Not that Dr. Lind's words were everywhere ignored, however, for some few far-sighted captains took them to heart at once. Among these was Captain James Cook, who preparing for his famous round-the-world expedition in 1768 stocked enough lemon juice to give his men a daily ration throughout the voyage—and he had not a case of scurvy in his crew, a fantastic record in those days. For this remarkable achievement, not for his feat of circumnavigating[5] the globe, he—and not Dr. Lind—received the gold medal of the Royal Society on his return.

Not for many years would anybody know why lemon juice would prevent scurvy or cure it so fast. Or why some fresh foods were more effective than others in stopping the disease. Not for more than a century would scurvy be recognized as a *vitamin deficiency disease*—one of a group of seemingly unrelated ailments which are quite unlike each other in their symptoms, but alike because they are all caused by the lack of one or another of the vitamins. For not till 1912 would a Polish-born chemist working in London discover the existence of the substances now so widely known as vitamins—*substances found in many common foods which, in tiny quantities, are essential for life and growth.*

---

4. hidebound: unwilling to change
5. circumnavigating: sailing all the way around

From *The Miracle of Vitamins,* by Doris Faber

The Time
of Your Life

Patty DiRienzo

Do you wake up before the alarm clock goes off? Why do you think this happens? Read this selection to find out about the natural clocks within living things and how these time systems can affect bodies and minds.

Listen to your own thoughts. Listen to people talking to each other.

"What day of the week is your birthday this year?"

"The time went so fast I was afraid I wasn't going to finish the book, but I did make enough time to write the report."

"I've got spring fever!"

"The beat and rhythm are the big things. You have to keep time when you dance."

"For everything there is a season, and a time for every matter under heaven …"

"What time is it?"

You can hear how important time is to us and how much attention we pay to hours and days and seasons and rhythms and cycles. We seem to have an inborn urge to keep pace with time.

In experiments during which, for a few days, people could only guess what time it was, they felt as if they were floating on a vast ocean without a compass. Why is *time* so strangely interesting and necessary to us?

I suppose no one really knows when humans began to keep track of the passing of time and to think about living their days and years in rhythm with the turning of the earth. But people were keeping time inwardly long before they noticed it.

As humans began to divide time into various pieces and to give the sections names, they gradually contrived an assortment of systems and gadgets to help them. One by one they tried out sundials, arrangements of burning candles, water clocks, sandglasses, and finally mechanical clocks.

Somewhere along the way people noticed that animals and birds seemed to have their own special timetables, some of them apparently in rhythm with changes in the moon or tides or seasons. Rather recently as history goes, the special curiosity of scientists was drawn to strange animal senses. People began to look at living rhythms and timetables from new and precise viewpoints.

The biologists are finding that life is a marvelously complex pattern of rhythms and time cycles, in tune with a world made up of the rhythmic movements of the sun, moon, stars, and planets and the precision of vibrating atoms.[1]

For instance, did you wake up on time this morning without the help of an alarm clock or some rousing music on the clock radio? Some persons seem to be able to do this every day, and nearly anyone can do it on special occasions.

When you go to bed planning to get up at seven o'clock the next morning so that you can leave on a vacation trip, you probably wake up a few minutes before seven, don't you? It is almost as if an alarm clock had rung inside your head.

In fact, scientists are concluding that probably all forms of life have built-in clocks of one kind or another. Even the very small individual cells that fit together to make up everything from pond slime to elephants

---

1. **atoms:** the tiny "building blocks" of all things

The rhythms of the moon and tides seem to affect living things. The moon circles the earth once in about 29½ days. The tides rise and fall twice between moonrises.

run on their own miniature timetables and calendars. Although it isn't easy to understand just how it is done, the chemical activities of the cells, plus special functions in the brain, may be at least part of the "works" of human and animal clocks. The "hands" of these clocks apparently are set and reset by changes from darkness to daylight and back again.

We know now that living things had to develop some sort of time system in order to survive at all. Without such a living clock-computer, a luna moth might leave its cocoon in the middle of a blizzard. Honeybees would hunt aimlessly for nectar, often too early or too late to find any. Animals, birds, and fish would migrate in haphazard directions if they got around to traveling at all, and they might be trying to raise their young at seasons of the year when bad weather and lack of food could kill them.

Human beings would be feeling miserable a good deal of the time, for many of the functions of their bodies would be running askew. The schedules of various organs and processes are different from each other, but they must all mesh together in one smoothly running system. When some of these rhythms become off balance—because of sudden changes such as those we experience when we fly to the other side of the world—we often feel tired and dull and even irritable. Some kinds of shocks that upset our normal cycles can make us seriously ill.

It is particularly urgent for space scientists to know what daily, monthly, and yearly rhythms exist in human beings. Their investigations must determine whether such cycles will continue to run in outer space

Flying through several time zones can upset the rhythms of the human body. If it is 10:27 P.M. Monday in Tokyo, it is 8:27 A.M. Monday in New York and 1:27 A.M. Monday in London.

during long voyages of exploration. All the indications are that human rhythms will continue to run and that astronauts will not be able to perform properly unless their schedules of rest and work are planned with these rhythms in mind.

Body temperature, blood pressure, heart rate, red and white blood cell counts, the amount of sugar in the blood, the chemistry of blood and urine, and the rate of cell division are some of the functions that have their ups and downs during each day and night. We perform at our best during the hours when our temperature is highest, usually in the afternoon—to mention just one interesting bit of information from the growing files of research.

We become particularly aware of our "bioclocks" when we take a trip in a jet plane. If you live in New York, for instance, and you usually wake up about 7:00 A.M., you are very likely to find yourself waking up at four o'clock the morning after a flight to San Francisco. If you stay a few days and eat your meals, go to bed, and get up when California people do, your sleep clock will reset itself from Eastern Standard Time to Pacific Standard Time. However, some of the inner clocks that control your temperature, blood pressure, and that sort of less obvious activity, may not reset themselves for a week or two. Until they are all on California time, your body will not be working as well as it usually does.

When people fly through several time zones in a few hours, their rhythms can become even more offbeat. This is hardly surprising when you realize that a person can leave Paris right after supper and fly all the way to New York, only to find New Yorkers just finishing their dinner. No wonder it takes a week or so to get over feeling a bit edgy, moody to the point of tears or senseless laughter, and sleepy and hungry at the wrong times.

Even more importantly, new tests are showing that mental abilities are thrown out of kilter for a day or so after such a flight. Highly educated men suddenly find it difficult to concentrate, to do simple arithmetic correctly, and to make decisions with their usual speed and good judgment. Most jet-flying diplomats and business executives, with many trips to make to the far side of the globe, now plan to rest for a day or two after arrival before taking part in important conferences when they must be at their best.

When supersonic[2] aircraft become normal transportation, more tests and still greater adjustments will almost surely be necessary. No one really knows what will happen to our normal cycles and reactions when we can fly at two or three thousand miles an hour to have lunch in England, and then return home to attend an afternoon meeting. Some researchers have suggested that short periods of light and darkness might help such travelers—and today's jet travelers, as well—to get their time systems back to normal.

Space scientists are puzzling over what long periods of weightlessness will do to the bioclocks of future astronauts, already mixed up by the timelessness of life in a spaceship. Perhaps artificial days and nights will have to be created in spacecraft to keep the voyagers' inner timekeepers synchronized[3] and to prevent serious effects on their brains and nervous systems. Since weightlessness makes muscles less tired, less sleep is needed during space flights. So astronauts may be able to stay awake and alert for longer periods. They might divide the time into 18-hour "days" or perhaps 28-hour ones, for such days should be much easier to manage in space than on the spinning earth.

Many scientists believe that when astronauts can travel at a good fraction of the speed of light, mechanical clock time in the spaceship and the living clocks of the astronauts will slow down. If that does happen, all the body processes of the astronauts will run more slowly too, of course, and very little food would be necessary for a trip that would last many years of earth time.

The fascinating question is whether the space travelers actually will age more slowly—and what then happens when they return to earth?

2. **supersonic:** traveling faster than the speed of sound
3. **synchronized:** agreeing in time

From *Biological Clocks and Patterns,* by Shirley Moore

Genetic Challenge

What are some of the physical characteristics that run in your family? People get their hair color, eye color, and many other traits from the genes their parents pass on. In some cases, people may also inherit birth defects. Read to find out what researchers are learning about genes, and think about some of the decisions we all may be facing in the future.

●■●■●■●■●■●■●■●■

Probably your parents worried a bit, now and then, before you were born. Were you developing normally or might something go wrong? Chances are that when you finally made your entrance into the world, your parents could breathe a sigh of relief: you had the usual number of fingers and toes; your eyes and nose and mouth were all present; you were a breathing, crying little human being.

For most parents, a normal baby is the happy result of pregnancy, and the long months of waiting and worrying are quickly forgotten. For about three in 100, though, birth may reveal problems. These babies are born with birth defects, some of which are hereditary.[1]

About 3,500 genetic disorders are now known—conditions that can be passed on from one generation to another, inherited by children from their parents. Some of them are obvious at birth, such as a jaw or skull that did not form properly. Disorders of the body chemistry are more subtle and may not be discovered until the child becomes ill or does not learn or grow as quickly as he or she should. Some hereditary disorders are like time bombs, lying undiscovered for years until they suddenly burst out—perhaps at adolescence or even in middle age.

---

1. hereditary: transmitted from parent to child by genes

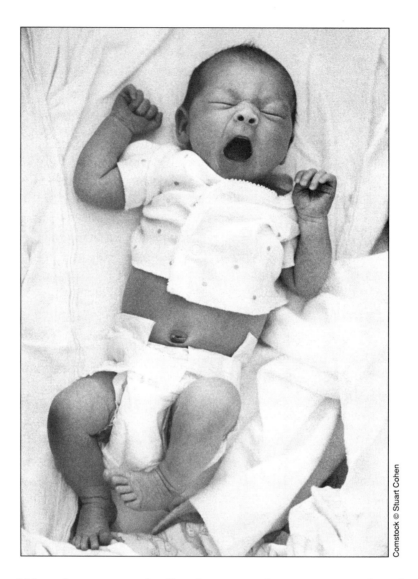

Although most genetic disorders are rather rare, researchers have discovered that heredity also plays a role in our susceptibility[2] to many common diseases. These include infectious diseases, such as tuberculosis, and even the major killers, cancer and heart disease. Genetic factors also have been implicated[3] in some forms of mental illness, as well as in drug abuse and alcoholism. Therefore, it's not surprising that major efforts in medical research have been focused on genetics—learning about how the instructions for forming and operating

---

2. susceptibility: level of ability to get or be affected by
3. implicated: shown to play a part in; involved

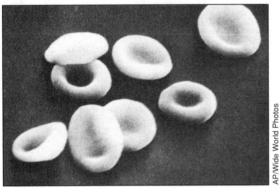

In sickle cell anemia, an inherited disease, red blood cells change into slender, sickle-shaped forms like those in the top photo. The bottom photo shows cells that have been treated with medicine and are nearly back to their normal, doughnut-like shape.

a complex human being are coded and stored inside tiny chemical structures so small that they cannot be seen without a powerful microscope. Researchers have been learning about genes, these tiny units of heredity, and the controls that turn them on and off according to the body's needs. They have made giant strides in recent decades. Geneticists, scientists who study heredity, can now identify many of the genes associated with particular traits—from the color of a person's eyes to a tendency for blood cells to collapse abruptly into a sickle-shaped form. Progress in identifying genes linked with inherited disorders has been so rapid in the past few years that one researcher was prompted to joke about the "gene of the week." Artificial genes have been made in the laboratory, and genes have been transferred from one organism to another.

New knowledge and skills have made it possible to test for genetic disorders in newborn babies or in a fetus[4] developing in its mother's womb. For some genetic conditions there are tests to identify carriers of the trait—people who may show no signs of the disorder themselves but might have children at risk. In a few cases, knowledge of the chemical basis of genetic disorders has suggested treatments to permit people born with them to live a relatively normal life. Babies born with a condition called PKU,[5] for example, used to be doomed to become mentally retarded. But simple and relatively inexpensive tests, which can be run routinely after birth, can detect PKU, and then a special diet can prevent

---

4. **fetus:** in humans, stage of development between three months and birth
5. **PKU:** abbreviation for phenylketonuria; a hereditary disease that can harm mental and physical growth

the buildup of poisons that could damage the baby's developing brain. In the future—perhaps not too far down the road—scientists hope to be able to go further. They are boldly planning ways to repair or replace defective genes—to tackle the causes of genetic disorders rather than just treat their symptoms.

The growing capabilities of genetic medicine have brought with them new responsibilities, social problems, and ethical dilemmas. Couples planning to marry or preparing to have a child may face agonizing choices if they find they are carrying potentially dangerous genes. Screening tests for genetic disorders can have enormous benefits, but they can also be misused to discriminate against groups of people. Doctors and researchers, as well as the community at large, must balance tricky equations of benefit and risk in their efforts to determine whether promising new techniques are ready for use on human patients.

Our past experiments in genetic tinkering—using techniques of animal and plant breeding before researchers developed the ability to splice genes[6]—have not been uniformly successful. And some of our most brilliant successes have proven to have unexpected drawbacks.

Plant breeders have developed new crop strains that were much hardier than natural varieties and gave vastly increased yields. Farmers enthusiastically adopted them—and then saw their whole crop wiped out a few years later by a new fungus disease or a shift in weather patterns. The new plants were too specialized and lost their survival advantage when conditions changed. When we gain the ability to change our own genome[7] at will, we may need to curb our enthusiasm. If everyone jumps on the bandwagon and incorporates an attractive new modification, we may rob the human genetic stock of the natural variability our species may some day need to survive.

If all plants in a crop were bred to have the same special traits, there might not be any that could adapt to something new in the environment such as a fungus disease.

---

6. splice genes: combine genetic information from two or more living things
7. genome: set of genes found in one sex cell (half the number of genes needed to form a complete being)

It could be argued that if environmental conditions change and we need new combinations of genes, we can use genetic engineering techniques to produce them. But too great a dependence on high-tech solutions may leave us dangerously vulnerable to some future catastrophe. Fortunately, it is unlikely that enough people will be able to agree on what changes are desirable to seriously reduce our genetic variability.

Who is to decide just what changes in the human genome are really improvements and which ones should be incorporated, if we gain the knowledge and skills to do so? Scientists sometimes tend to get carried away with enthusiasm for their work and are not always the most objective judges of what is prudent. But politicians do not have a very good track record for making ethical decisions, either. And the idea of making genetic improvements brings uncomfortable memories of the "eugenic"[8] experiments in Nazi Germany, where the "final solution" was applied to millions of people judged to be inferior, and a misguided Lebensborn project attempted to breed perfect Aryans.[9] It is not surprising that the average person views the potentials of genetic engineering with hope and also with some gut-level misgivings.

In a 1985 Harris poll sponsored by *Business Week,* about two-thirds of those questioned answered yes when asked if treatments altering genes to cure people with fatal diseases should be allowed to go ahead. Nearly as many agreed that if they were found to be carriers of a genetic disease and could have their genes altered to protect their children and future generations, they would do so. But the idea of altering genes to improve one's children—to make them smarter, physically stronger, or better looking—made them pause. A resounding 88 percent felt that would be going too far.

---

8. eugenic: dealing with the improvement of the hereditary traits of a race or breed
9. Aryans: peoples of Germany and other regions of northern Europe whom the Nazis claimed were members of a superior race

---

From *Genes, Medicine, and You,* by Alvin and Virginia Silverstein

How do you react to spiders? Not everyone views spiders with fear. In some places, people consider them food. Read to learn more about these creatures and how useful they can be to humans.

Who Needs *Spiders?*

If you had been in the rice and cotton fields of China in the fall of 1988, you might have seen a strange sight: farmers building little tepees out of straw. But even though the conical huts—about waist-high and scattered across thousands of acres—looked bizarre, they had a serious purpose: to house hibernating spiders.

Normally, winter kills most spiders, and it takes months for the population to recover. But that spring occupants of the spider motels awakened from hibernation healthy and ravenous. They scuttled into the fields in hordes, ready to attack the insects attempting to suck the life out of the young rice and cotton plants. By protecting the spiders and giving them an early start, the Chinese increased their crop yields and avoided having to use chemical insecticides.

Although the Chinese were the first to harness spider power on a grand scale, agricultural experts in America and other countries have caught on and now are beginning to pamper spiders too.

Pictured is a wolf spider. Try to find its eight eyes, which are on the top and near the front of its head.

Often mistaken for insects,[1] spiders actually belong to a different classification of creatures, called arachnids.[2] They are insects' worst enemies, killing far more pests than commercial insecticides do. According to one estimate, spiders devour enough bugs worldwide in a single day to outweigh the entire human population.

Pest control, we are learning, is just one of the many ways spiders can help us. Already they're being studied in connection with possible drugs for brain disorders. Before long, they may be used in applications as diverse as surgical implants and bulletproof vests.

Willard H. Whitcomb, emeritus professor of entomology[3] at the University of Florida, has been singing the praises of spiders for decades. Called the Florida Spiderman by admiring colleagues, Whitcomb has diligently turned up many of their useful talents.

One type of banana spider, for instance, is a little, brownish-gray creature, which is usually harmless to humans and lives in warm climates. It loves cockroaches, and can keep a house clear of these hated insects. "In Central America," says Whitcomb, "the banana spider is a welcome house guest. It eats insects and some small lizards that crawl on the walls— anything the homemaker hates."

Whitcomb also has worked with wolf spiders, a common field variety averaging about the diameter of a quarter. He found that leaving strips of weeds around soybean and cotton fields fosters the kind of undergrowth favored by wolf spiders, which will then patrol the fields—for free.

At the University of California at Berkeley, Professor Miguel Altieri plants ground cover between the trees in abandoned apple orchards. This prompts a dramatic rise in the spider population—and dooms many of the little moths whose larvae[4] become the "worms" in bad apples. Altieri estimates that 22 percent more of his crop now is of marketable quality.

In Texas, Marvin Harris, a professor at Texas A&M University, has found that spiders can control aphids in pecan orchards. "Unlike ladybugs, wasps, and other natural enemies that fly away if the

1. **insects:** small animals with no backbones, six legs, and bodies divided into three main sections
2. **arachnids:** small animals with no backbones, eight legs, and bodies divided into two sections
3. **entomology:** branch of science that involves the study of insects
4. **larvae:** the wormlike young forms of insects that change to become adults

hunting turns poor, spiders apparently sit and starve for weeks, waiting for food to come," says Harris. As a result, they clean up many insect problems before the farmer even notices.

In Maine, Daniel Jennings of the U.S. Forest Service has enlisted spiders in the war against the spruce budworm, the Northeast's most devastating enemy of spruce and fir forests. Because each spider can eat five or six budworms a day, a legion of spiders can play a major role in preventing an infestation[5] from developing. Spiders also attack the much-feared gypsy moth.

Although a few species of spiders are dangerous, such as the black widow and the brown recluse, the vast majority are harmless to humans. Reports of spider bites are greatly exaggerated. One check of 600 cases in California revealed that 80 percent were probably caused by insects.

Bugs, however, have every reason to fear spiders, for they have developed incredibly ingenious hunting methods—spitting, for instance. Spitting spiders are so lethargic[6] that you'd swear they could never catch anything. But when one of them creeps close to a fly—the usual target—its body jerks and a gob of spit

shoots out so fast the fly cannot react. Suddenly the fly finds itself pinned under a downpour of glue, as if in a Roman centurion's net. The happy spider then saunters over and finishes the job with the paralyzing venom in its fangs.

Spider venoms are exquisitely refined to interfere with the nervous systems of insects. They alter the chemical that bridges the gap between the victim's nerve endings and its muscles. After a spider bite, an insect's brain continues to telegraph messages down to its nerves, but the instructions never get delivered to the muscles. The insect is powerless to move while the spider eats it alive.

That's a chilling thought, but not for us. In fact, some components of the venom may *benefit* human health. At least one group of researchers is testing spider chemicals in drugs to combat epilepsy and Alzheimer's disease.

Web-weaving spiders are deadly hunters too. The triangle spider, for example, builds a triangular web, and like a boy tugging on a slingshot, pulls the whole assemblage taut. When an insect strikes the web, the spider lets go and the web snaps back and wraps around the victim. The purse-web spider spins a silken tube like a crooked finger of a glove sticking out of the ground. The spider lurks inside the dense silken screen, and when an insect crawls over the outer surface, the spider bites

---

5. **infestation:** harmfully large number
6. **lethargic:** slow-moving

through—and suddenly the insect finds jaws attached to its feet.

What interests scientists about web-weaving spiders is the silk strands of the webs. Because each strand is so fine, spider silk seems very weak. In fact, some types are stronger than steel. Particularly tough is "dragline silk," which supports the spider as it hangs in front of your face or rides the winds in search of greener pastures.

At least three spiders produce dragline silk that, if spun into thicker strands, could be as strong as the nylon and carbon fibers used in high-performance aircraft. Furthermore, dragline silk is elastic, which many of the synthetic fibers are not.

Protein Polymer Technologies, Inc., in San Diego is working extensively with spider silk, and company officials believe the material will be used one day in heart valves, artificial veins, and other surgical implants.

The U.S. Army has gotten into the act too. At its Research, Development & Engineering Center in Natick, Massachusetts, biochemist David Kaplan and colleagues hope to copy a spider silk to make a bulletproof vest that is lighter and more comfortable than the stiff Kevlar vests now worn by police and soldiers.

Spider ranching may never overtake cattle ranching, but there is at least one spider that supplies food. Found in the jungles of New Guinea, *Nephila maculata* spins enormous circular webs, bigger than bicycle wheels. And the female—300 times larger than the male and big enough to cover the palm of a person's hand—is edible.

"People gather fat females in a hollow green bamboo stick," explains Michael Robinson, director of the National Zoo in Washington, D.C. "They stopper both ends and place the stick in hot embers for 10 or 15 minutes, until it blackens. When they take the roasted spiders out, the hard skins have split and they're ready to eat—with or without legs.

"The New Guineans taught me to eat it," Robinson adds. "Its not like shrimp … more like peanut butter, but I guess you'd have to say it's a very acquired taste!"

The future probably won't see spiders served at our tables. But perhaps if our farmers employ armies of spiders to protect their fields, our grocery bills will be lower and our soil and water and food will have fewer pesticide residues.

"Who Needs Spiders?" by Noel Vietmeyer, from *Reader's Digest*

Have you been to a zoo recently? If so, what did you get out of your visit? Zoos have changed a lot in the last 20 years. Read to find out how the new zoos are part of a larger movement to save species and habitats.

The New Zoo:

A Modern Ark

Call it a natural disaster. The San Diego Zoo spent $3.5 million to build a designer forest that would house five adolescent Malayan sun bears. The zookeepers planted some trees, dug a moat, launched a waterfall, even hooked up a fiber-glass tree with an electric honey dispenser. As company for their wards,[1] they invited lion-tailed macaques, yellow-breasted laughing thrushes, orange-bellied fruit doves, and Indian pigmy geese.

When the lush exhibit opened this summer, zoogoers loved it. So did the bears. They shredded the trees, rolled up the sod, plugged the moat—and then one attempted a fast break over the wall. Spectators went scrambling for a zookeeper, who propped up a plywood barrier while another clanged some pots and pans to intimidate the beasts and herd them into a locked enclosure.

Meanwhile, at Washington's National Zoo another experiment was under way: scientists wanted to acquaint their rare golden lion tamarins with a facsimile[2] of their natural habitat, a lowland Brazilian forest. But the coddled, zoo-happy monkeys lacked some basic skills—how, for instance, to peel a banana. Instead, they fell out of the trees and got lost in the woods.

At some 150 American zoos in between, the troubles are not very

---

1. **wards:** beings who are under the care of others
2. **facsimile:** copy or likeness

White-handed gibbons on an artificial island in an Oregon zoo. Instead of using walls and bars, a moat keeps the animals from wandering off.

different. The sharks eat the angelfish. The Australian hairy-nosed wombat stays in its cave, and the South American smoky jungle frog hunkers down beneath a leaf, all tantalizingly hidden from the prying eyes of the roughly 110 million Americans who go to zoos every year. Visitors often complain that as a result of all the elaborate landscaping, they cannot find the animals. But this, like almost everything else that goes wrong these days, is a signal that America's zoos are doing something very right.

Just about every aspect of America's zoos has dramatically changed—and improved—from what viewers saw a generation ago. Gone are the sour cages full of frantic cats and the concrete tubs of thawing penguins. Instead the terrain is uncannily authentic, and animals are free to behave like, well, animals, not inmates. Here is a Himalayan highland full of red pandas, there a subtropical jungle where it rains indoors, 11 times a day. The effect is of an entire globe miraculously concentrated, the wild kingdom contained in downtown Chicago or the North Bronx. As American zoos are renovated and redesigned—at a cost of more than a billion dollars since 1980—hosts of once jaded visitors, some even without children, are flooding through the gates. "In the past 15 years," says Cincinnati zoo director Edward Maruska, "we've probably changed more than we've changed in the past hundred."

And all to what end? To entertain, of course, but to do more than that. By junking the cages and building vast biological gardens, the zoos provide a decent, delightful place for animals and people to meet and, with luck, fall in love. Once that bond is made, the visitors discover there is a larger mission at hand, a crusade to join. Between the birth of Christ and the Pilgrims' landing, perhaps several species a year became extinct. By the 1990s the extinction rate may reach several species an hour, around the clock. American zoos are leading the battle to stop that clock and recruit others to the preservationist's cause. "We don't just want you to come here," says David Anderson of the New Orleans Audubon Park. "We're trying to say, 'Do something!' "

The zoos have therefore taken on a role as educators that dwarfs that of any other "recreational" institution. Whole public school systems are redesigning their science curriculums to take advantage of local exhibits, for what better biology classroom could there be than a swamp or a rain forest? The newest facilities, such as the Living World in St. Louis, include state-of-the-art computer technology that turns a simple menagerie[3] into a cross between a laboratory and a video arcade.

Though highly effective at raising consciousness and making converts, this is not an easy or a cheap way to run a zoo. At the Tiger River exhibit in San Diego, that lovely gushing waterfall is part of a 72,000-gallon computerized irrigation system. A huge banyan tree has heating coils in its roots to encourage the python to uncoil near the viewing glass. Not far away, an agile cliff-springer mountain goat is contained on the assumption that it will not jump eight feet to a ledge on the moat's far side that is constructed at a precise 30° angle. "But," admits architect David Rice, "nobody has told the cliff springer that."

Beyond the aesthetic[4] and mechanical challenges, there is the basic issue of what zoogoers should be allowed to see in a naturalistic setting. Zoo directors

AP/Wide World Photos

Zebras and a baby giraffe share a wide, open space in an animal park in California.

refer to "the Bambi syndrome," a belief common among visitors that all creatures should be cuddly, or at least not killers. A while back, the Detroit Zoo staff euthanatized[5] a dying goat from the children's zoo and placed it in the African-swamp exhibit, which includes big vultures. Doing what came naturally, the vultures ate the goat. About half the zoogoers who happened upon the scene were fascinated, says director Steve Graham. But the other half averted their children's eyes and scurried away.

---

3. menagerie: place where a collection of animals is kept for show
4. aesthetic: having to do with beauty or pleasing the senses; artistic
5. euthanatized: killed for reasons of mercy

Zoos can help children to respect and value the richness of the animal world.

For all the increased drama in the exhibits themselves, the real revolution is going on behind the scenes and out in the wild, where a state of emergency exists. To begin with, most zoos no longer take animals from the jungle; they grow their own. About 90 percent of the mammals and 75 percent of the birds now in United States zoos were bred in captivity, and some are even being carefully reintroduced to their native environs. At the same time, zoo-affiliated organizations like Wildlife Conservation International are working to save whole habitats in 38 countries in Africa, Asia, and South America and to reduce the threats to endangered species. Says the Bronx Zoo's visionary director William Conway: "Our objectives are very clear—to save fragments of nature, to preserve biodiversity.[6]"

As zoos fight back, they are pulling along the public with some shrewd tactics. Conservationists[7] often select an irresistible, oversize crowd pleaser—pandas are perfect, but snow leopards and black rhinos work fine—and lead a campaign to preserve the creature's habitat. "There is a utility[8] in the concern for the giant panda," says the National Zoo's director Michael Robinson. "Pandas are relatively stupid and uninteresting animals. But they happen to be photogenic and appealing, and they help focus people's attention." Big animals need big swatches of habitat, and so in the process a lot of less sexy species are protected too. To save the African elephant requires saving the Serengeti.[9] That means roughly 5,000 square miles and, as it happens, 400 species of birds, maybe 50 species of mammals,[10] and tens of thousands of invertebrates.[11] And the elephants.

Though many of these outlying efforts have been wildly successful, the zoos themselves are still the front line. A child who rubs noses, even through the plate glass, with a polar bear or a penguin may be far more likely to mature into an eager conservationist than into one who sees animals as toys or accessories. It is hard to walk around a good zoo without caring, deeply, about whether this miraculous wealth of lovely, peculiar, creepy, unfathomable creatures survives or perishes. And it will be a great sorrow if zoos are ever the last place on earth where the wild things are.

---

6. **biodiversity:** variety in the world of life
7. **conservationists:** persons who work to protect our natural resources
8. **utility:** usefulness
9. **Serengeti:** area of land in Northern Tanzania in Central Africa
10. **mammals:** animals with backbones and hair that feed their young with milk
11. **invertebrates:** animals that do not have backbones

"The New Zoo: A Modern Ark," by Nancy Gibbs, from *Time*

Unit 2: Physics

*the science that deals with the properties
and interrelationships of matter and energy*

TWITTERING MACHINE, 1922, Paul Klee, watercolor and pen and ink on oil transfer
drawing on paper, mounted on cardboard, 25$\frac{1}{4}$" x 19". Collection, The Museum of Modern Art,
New York. Purchase.

What do you think it would be like if you could shrink to a few inches and explore the inside of a computer? A museum in Boston, Massachusetts, decided to give people a way to find out. Instead of making visitors smaller, the museum built a huge model computer. As you read, imagine yourself inside this exhibit.

This Is Big. Reeeeally Big.

For years, the goal in computing has been to make things smaller, building down from early room-size monsters to today's palmtop PCs. Even computer terms—like "bit" and "microprocessor"—connote tininess. Now The Computer Museum, Boston's repository of vintage number-crunchers[1] and intriguing interactive[2] exhibits, has gone the other way: a really, really BIG computer, two stories tall. It boasts keys a foot across, six-foot-wide disks, and—get ready for this oxymoron[3]—the biggest microchip in the world, $7^1/_2$ feet square. The Walk-Through Computer, a new permanent exhibit modeled after such displays as the walk-through human heart at Chicago's Museum of Science and Industry, will give visitors a chance to see the soul of a new machine close up. No wonder the museum is calling the June 21, 1990, unveiling "the biggest event in computer history." Steve Jobs,[4] eat your heart out.

From the outside, the machine looks like most any PC with a pituitary[5] condition. It will even run a program—World Traveler—designed by museum staffers. Using the gargantuan[6]

---

1. **vintage number-crunchers:** old, important, or classic computers and earlier counting machines
2. **interactive:** involving communication back and forth between people and machines
3. **oxymoron:** figure of speech in which opposites are used; a seeming contradiction
4. **Steve Jobs:** co-inventor of the Apple computer
5. **pituitary:** gland that produces a substance that causes growth
6. **gargantuan:** huge

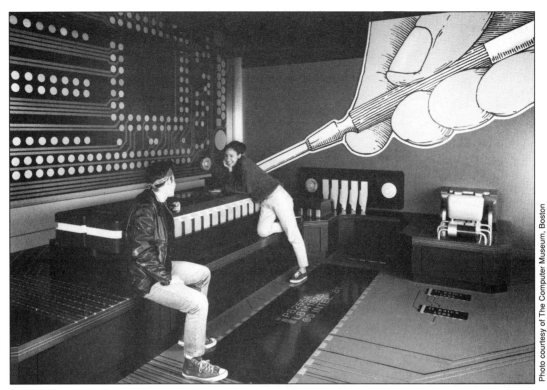

Inside the Walk-Through Computer™ at The Computer Museum, Boston

keys and a pointing device known as a trackball—this one measures almost 10 feet by 7 feet—visitors choose two spots on a map. The computer figures the shortest route between the two cities and flashes pictures of sights along the way—say, San Francisco's Golden Gate Bridge, or Amarillo's Cadillac Ranch. The trackball, keyboard, and screen are connected to an Apple Macintosh squirreled away backstage that does the actual computing. A Digital Equipment Corp. computer controls special effects.

After fiddling with the program, visitors can enter the chassis[7] and walk from component to component, guided by the circuitry itself and illustrations by David Macaulay, author of the best-selling *The Way Things Work*. Each part of the machine tells its own story. At the center of the board lies the microprocessor "brain," a replica of the Intel 486 found in today's most powerful PCs. Looking into a window on the chip, visitors will see a hugely enlarged picture of the actual lines etched in the silicon. That image fades, and computer-produced artwork takes over, zooming down to the surface for a step-by-step animated[8] portrayal of the chip's operation—the tiny mundane steps that it accomplishes millions of times each second, such as asking the memory for a chunk of data and shooting

---

7. chassis: outer frame
8. animated: seeming to move

Oliver Strimpel, executive director of The Computer Museum, Boston, got the idea for the exhibit.

Jack McWilliams Photography © 1990

that information out to the screen. That image is in turn replaced by footage taken by a scanning electron microscope[9] which shows a real 486 chip at work. (Since the microscope's image is made up of electrons, it can "see" the changes in voltage[10] along the chip.) Beyond the PC itself, a video "software theater" explains the way the computer's programming interacts with the hardware. So that visitors could learn as much or as little as they wish, the designers kept as their motto, "Simple message, rich context." A bank of terminals on the way out of the exhibit

allows even further delving into the arcana[11] of computing.

The elegant idea is the brainchild of the museum's executive director, Oliver Strimpel, who has been working on the $1.2 million exhibit for three years. Despite the expense, Strimpel found it the easiest sell of his career. "It clicked immediately with everyone," he says, glowing. "Everyone said, 'Of course! You've got to do that.'"

'Make it sing':

Putting it together hasn't been quite as easy. Even though the museum staff had decided from the beginning that their mock-up computer would not actually perform the computations, they wanted verisimilitude[12]—a computer that *could* work. The museum took on the extra challenge to satisfy the technologically demanding Route 128[13] crowd. "We believe that authenticity is what's really going to make it sing for the technical people," Strimpel says. So they turned to a group of companies that design computer boards. Creating the main board, or "motherboard," usually takes two weeks, but this job took two months. The designers faced unusual constraints, says museum spokesperson Gail Jennes: "They not only had to worry about how to move data around, they also had to move people around." (To get to the men's room, you have to

---

9. **scanning electron microscope:** a type of microscope that enlarges tiny images using a beam of electrons, which are smaller than atoms; the electron beam scans an object in order to produce an image on a TV screen
10. **voltage:** force of electric power
11. **arcana:** secrets; mysteries
12. **verisimilitude:** appearance of reality
13. **Route 128 crowd:** people who work in the computer industry of Massachusetts (Route 128 refers to a highway outside of Boston.)

walk through the "power supply.") Now "it can work," says Donald Glass, whose company, DGA Associates, coordinated the design effort and had several small-scale models with real chips made for the museum. He admits DGA stopped short of a thorough debugging. "I just hope they don't plug it in."

All right, so we all agree it's cool. But what else? Strimpel says the Big Box should fulfill one of the first missions of the museum, which is to demystify computing. "Any place you've been is less of a mystery than any place you haven't been," Strimpel says.

It should thrill kids and satisfy inquisitive[14] adults. Once visitors have ventured into this cross between "Fantastic Voyage" and "Land of the Giants,[15]" they will know more about computers—as much as most would ever want to know. So the big computer will have done something that its pygmy brethren[16] have so far found nearly impossible: making learning fun.

---

14. **inquisitive:** curious; questioning
15. **"Fantastic Voyage" and "Land of the Giants":** two science-fiction productions—one in which people are tiny and one in which people are huge
16. **pygmy brethren:** small relatives

Do you know these computer words?

board: short for circuit board; where the chips are located

debugging: correcting mistakes in a computer program

disks: round pieces of plastic with magnetic surfaces, sealed in square envelopes and used to store data

hardware: the physical items that make up a computer system—the central processing unit (CPU), memory chips, keyboard, screen, and so on

keyboard: input device that is similar to a typewriter keyboard

microchip: an incredibly small piece of silicon that holds the circuitry needed to make a computer work

microprocessor: the central processing unit, stored on a single silicon chip

motherboard: the main circuit board of a computer

PC: abbreviation for personal computer

program: list of instructions for the computer

screen: part that displays the computer's video output

silicon: an abundant element that is the main ingredient of sand; in melted form it is used to make computer chips

software: the programs run by the computer

terminals: usually having keyboards and screens, the means by which people and computers communicate

trackball: a pointing device that allows computer users to change their position on the screen

---

"This Is Big. Reeeeally Big," by John Schwartz, from *Newsweek*

Do you know the magician's trick in which a tablecloth is pulled off a table, leaving all the dishes, silver, and glassware in place? What do you think makes this trick work? Believe it or not, the trick shows a perfect example of Isaac Newton's First Law of Motion. Read to discover more about Newton's Laws of Motion.

UPI/Bettmann Archives

What Makes Things Move?

It's a little after dawn on a warm Florida morning. On a huge concrete platform supported by a towering steel gantry,[1] the Space Shuttle stands ready for takeoff. White plumes of vapor stream from vents in the smooth metal skin of the orbiter.[2] Everything is quiet. Then suddenly a tremendous shower of flame erupts from the shuttle's engines. Gradually at first, then faster and faster, the gigantic but graceful craft roars into the sky.

The Space Shuttle is a miracle of twentieth-century technology. It is built with hundreds of special materials, wired with the latest electronic computers, and equipped with the most effective life-support systems the National Aeronautic and Space Administration (NASA) can devise. But

---

1. gantry: movable framework used to service rockets when they are pointed upward
2. orbiter: the part of the space shuttle that carries astronauts and cargo and that returns to Earth at the end of a mission

the natural laws that explain how the shuttle takes off, moves through the earth's atmosphere, and orbits the earth were all discovered almost 300 years ago. They were all discovered by the man who may have been *the* greatest scientist who ever lived, Isaac Newton.

When the Space Shuttle leaps into orbit, or when anything else in our universe moves, it moves according to the laws that Newton discovered and wrote down in the late 1600s.

The universe is filled with moving objects. Wheels roll, birds and planes fly, trees sway in the breeze. Basketballs bounce, kites soar, boats sail, and people walk. Our earth and other planets in the solar system move. So do the moon, the sun, other stars, and even galaxies. What do all the various motions in the universe have in common? Are there any rules to describe how and why objects move?

The study of how things move is called *mechanics*. Archimedes[3] studied the mechanics of simple machines like levers and wheels. Galileo[4] studied mechanics when he experimented with falling objects. But it was the English scientist Isaac Newton who made the most complete discoveries about moving objects.

Think about what happens when a ball is rolled down a ramp onto a perfectly flat surface. It continues to roll, although after a while, it will slow to a stop. Early natural philosophers,[5] followers of Aristotle,[6] believed that the ball would need a continuous force pushing on it to keep it rolling. They thought that when the force was "used up," the ball would stop rolling.

Galileo realized that once a ball starts rolling, no more force is needed to keep it rolling. Galileo also realized that it is air resistance[7] and friction (rubbing) against the surface on which the ball is rolling that finally make it stop.

What if there were no friction or air resistance, Newton asked? What if there were nothing to slow the ball down once it starts moving? Newton realized that unless some force acts to slow the ball down, it will continue on forever!

Now suppose we place our ball on a perfectly flat surface and steady it so that it is perfectly still. Unless we use some kind of force, like a push or a puff of air, the ball will *stay* perfectly still. It will never move by itself.

---

3. Archimedes: scientist of ancient Greece in the 200s B.C. known for discovering many scientific principles
4. Galileo: Italian astronomer, mathematician, and physicist, living from 1564–1642
5. natural philosophers: persons who observe and try to explain events in nature
6. Aristotle: philosopher and teacher in Greece in the 300s B.C. who applied logic to the study of knowledge
7. air resistance: opposing force that air has

An object in motion continues in motion and an object at rest remains at rest unless acted upon by a force. What force sets a croquet ball into motion?

Newton understood that an object will change its motion only if it is acted upon by a force. Otherwise, its motion will be unchanged. If it is moving, it will continue to move in the same direction. And if it is standing still, it will remain still. That is Newton's First Law of Motion. It is usually stated as: An object in motion continues in motion and an object at rest remains at rest unless acted upon by a force.

This law is often called the law of inertia. *Inertia* is simply the scientific term for matter's property of continuing its motion (or lack of motion) until acted on by some force.

You can see Newton's First Law in action in the following demonstration: Get a drinking glass, a quarter, and a playing card. Place the card over the mouth of the glass and put the quarter in the middle of the card. Thanks to the law of inertia, it is possible to get the quarter into the glass without touching it. Simply flick the edge of the card with your fingernail. The card will go flying out, while the quarter will fall into the glass.

The trick works because an object at rest (the coin) remains at rest unless acted on by a force. Your finger provides enough force to make the card move. But a playing card is slippery and doesn't create much friction against the coin as it is flicked away. That means there isn't enough force acting on the heavy coin to get it moving very fast. As a result, the coin falls into the glass as the card is removed.

The famous trick in which a tablecloth is pulled off a table, leaving all the dishes, silver, and glassware in place, works exactly the same way. When the magician snaps the tablecloth away, all the dishes are at

What force or forces cause a croquet ball to stop moving?

rest. Because of Newton's First Law, they tend to remain at rest. The rapidly moving tablecloth doesn't produce enough force to move the dishes very much, and so they stay on the table. By the way, please don't try this trick at home. It takes lots of skill, heavy dishes, and a very slick tablecloth.

Objects moving in space have no air resistance or friction to slow them down. According to Newton's First Law, they should continue moving through space in a straight line forever. And that is exactly what happens. The *Voyager* satellites were launched into space in 1977. They carry messages of greeting from the people of our planet. Their rocket engines stopped burning long ago. But the *Voyagers* are still traveling through space, farther and farther from Earth. The *Voyagers* will continue on their journeys for millions of years, until something or someone stops them.

Newton's Second Law of Motion tells us how an object's motion changes when a force acts on it. To explain it clearly, we need to define two terms:

Mass is the amount of matter or substance an object is made of. (Notice that it is not the same thing as weight.[8])

Acceleration is any change in the motion of an object. It can be a change in speed (either slower or faster) or a change in direction. As Newton's First Law tells us, an object can't accelerate unless force is applied to it.

---

8. **weight:** how heavy a thing is

Now let's consider a situation from everyday life. Suppose your family's car has run out of gas on a level road. Up ahead is a gas station. All you have to do is push your car there.

One thing that you certainly know is that the harder you push, the faster your car will roll. If only one passenger leans against the back of the car, the car may start rolling, but it will move very slowly. And that one person will have to work very hard. But if three or four people push, the car will move much more easily. Why? Because four people can provide much greater force than one can. The greater the force applied to an object, the more it will accelerate.

Would it make a difference if your car were a small, lightweight compact or a heavy luxury sedan? Which would be easier to push? The smaller car would move more easily, of course. The more mass an object has, the more force needed to make it accelerate. A large luxury car has much more mass than a little economy model, and so it takes more effort to overcome its inertia and get it moving.

The acceleration (or change in motion) of an object depends on two things: the mass of the object and the amount of force applied. The more force that is used, the greater the acceleration. The more mass to be moved, the less acceleration you will get with an equal amount of force. Those are the two ideas of Newton's Second Law of Motion.

The Second Law of Motion is often known as the law of acceleration. It is usually stated like this: The acceleration of an object is directly proportional to the force applied to the object and inversely proportional to the mass of the object.

Before we go on, it's important that you understand what *directly proportional* and *inversely proportional* mean. They are not as difficult as they might sound.

If two measurements are *directly* proportional, then when one increases, the other increases too. For example, if you are driving at 50 miles per hour, the distance you cover is directly proportional to the amount of time you drive. As time increases, so does distance. The longer you drive, the farther you go.

In the example of the stalled car, the greater the force used to push it, the more the car will accelerate. Acceleration is directly proportional to the amount of force being used.

If two measurements are *inversely* proportional, then as one increases, the other decreases. For example, if you are taking a trip of 100

The more mass an object has, the more force needed to make it accelerate. Which car seems to have more mass? Which car seems to need more force to make it move?

miles, the time of the trip will be inversely proportional to the speed that you drive. The faster you drive, the shorter the time of the trip. As the speed increases, the time decreases.

We can see examples of the Second Law of Motion in action everywhere. When a batter swings and hits a baseball, the bat applies a force to the ball, changing its speed and direction. How far the ball goes depends on how much force is in the swing of the bat. Construction workers apply force as they move the steel girders they use to build skyscrapers and bridges. The more massive the girder, the more force needed to move it. The law explains why freight trains and jet airliners need such huge, powerful engines. It takes a tremendous amount of force to get all that mass moving!

Now let's look at Newton's Third Law of Motion. Picture a man paddling a canoe across a lake. Each time he takes a stroke with his paddle, he pushes some water toward the stern (rear) of the canoe. Each time he pushes this water *backward,* the canoe moves *forward.* Newton's Third Law of Motion is known as the law of action and reaction. It is usually stated like this: For every action, there is an equal, opposite reaction.

As our canoeist paddles across the lake, he is pushing the water behind him with his paddle. That is the action. The reaction is the canoe moving forward in the water, with the same amount of force that the paddler used in his stroke.

For every action there is an equal, opposite reaction. When a balloon is opened, it contracts and pushes air out of the opened end. What is the reaction to that force?

Newton's Third Law describes why a rifle recoils, or "kicks," when it is fired. As the bullet fires forward out of the gun barrel (action), the force of the reaction pushes the gun backward against the marksman's shoulder.

Whenever you see a rocket or jet take off, you are seeing Newton's Third Law in action. When a rocket or jet engine is ignited, a tremendous amount of force pushes hot gases out of the rear of the vehicle. Newton's Third Law tells us that there must be an equal amount of force to balance this in the opposite direction. In this case, that reaction results in the forward motion of the aircraft or rocket.

Here's how to make a simple demonstration of the Third Law with a drinking straw, a balloon, some tape, and a ball of string. Tie one end of a long piece of string to something sturdy. Tie it well above ground level. A tree trunk, lamppost, or doorknob will work well. Slip the string through a plastic drinking straw, pull the string tight, and tie the other end to another sturdy object. The string should be tight enough so that it doesn't sag in the middle. Slide the straw to one end of the string. Now inflate the balloon and close off the end with a short piece of string tied in a bow. Securely tape the inflated balloon to the straw. Now untie the bow holding the air in the balloon and watch your rocket take off.

Why does this work? The air is pushed out of the opened end of the balloon because of the force of the balloon's contraction. That is the action from Newton's Third Law. The balloon "rocket" moves forward along the string in the opposite direction, as a reaction to that force.

A Moving Frontier

The frontier of the science of physics is a boundary between the known and the unknown. It is a moving frontier. In every one of its divisions physicists keep pushing the frontier into new unexplored regions. Where they have studied small things, like atoms, they try to learn about smaller things. Where they have studied distant things, like galaxies, they try to learn about more distant ones. Having produced temperatures as low as .00001° Kelvin,[9] they try to produce lower temperatures. Having heated plasmas[10] to a temperature of millions of degrees, they try to make them hotter. Each advance of the frontier answers some old questions. But every new discovery raises new questions. Physicists will always have new regions of the unknown to explore.

From *The Wonders of Physics,* by Irving Adler

Perhaps you've seen plastic toy rockets that are designed to be filled with water and then pumped up with air pressure. When they are released, the air pressure forces the water out of the back of the rocket. The rocket leaps into the air as the water jets out the back. Of course, this toy works because of Newton's Third Law.

The Third Law is even at work when we walk down the street. Imagine what it would be like if, when we pushed against the earth with our feet, nothing pushed back. With no resistance, we'd never get anywhere! Fortunately, when we push against the earth with our feet, we do get resistance. Our muscles push against the earth (action), and our bodies move forward (reaction).

In addition to his discoveries about motion and gravitation, Newton also made important discoveries about light. He also invented a new kind of mathematics called calculus. Newton received many honors for his discoveries. The metric[11] unit used to measure force, called the newton, is named in his honor.

---

9. **Kelvin:** temperature scale that is the international standard for scientific temperature measurement; on this scale, 0° is absolute zero, which is believed to be the lowest temperature that can be reached
10. **plasmas:** collections of charged particles that are like gases in some ways but not in all ways
11. **metric:** of the system of measurement that uses the meter as its basic unit

---

From *Secrets of the Universe,* by Paul Fleisher

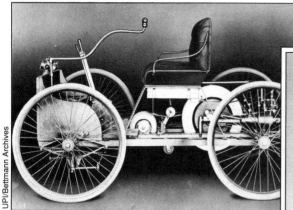

The first Ford motorcar

The supersonic Concorde

Tomorrow's Transportation

What kind of transportation do you think we'll have in the twenty-first century? Will it be faster? cleaner? safer? cheaper? Read this selection to find out what changes are already in the works.

Tomorrow, getting there could be a lot more than half the fun. To visit a friend across town, you might soar above the rooftops in your own lightweight aircraft. On a vacation trip, you could find yourself skimming along at 250 miles an hour (402 kilometers per hour, or km/h) aboard a train that doesn't touch the rails. These are just two of the many exciting things that are happening in the world of transportation. The changes are helping people go places

faster, with less expense, and often in greater comfort and safety.

Consider the modern airplane. In 1976, the first supersonic[1] jetliner, the Concorde, began scheduled passenger service. The Concorde streaks over the Atlantic at 1,350 miles an hour (2,173 km/h), twice the speed of sound. It flies from New York City to Paris, France, in only four hours. That's about half the

---

1. **supersonic:** traveling faster than the speed of sound

A 1992 Toyota Paseo

A driverless, computer-steered magnetic rail coach

time taken by standard jets such as the 747.

Designers want to do more than just make airplanes fly fast. For example, they're using new plastics and metals—strong but lightweight—to make planes more fuel-efficient. They're changing the shapes to make planes more maneuverable—able to turn and climb quickly in a small area.

Computers help run the world's largest machines: giant oil tankers. The largest tanker, the Liberian-registered *Seawise Giant,* is five times longer than a football field. You might think the ship would need an extra-large crew to handle it. It doesn't. Thanks to computers that do much of the work, the crew numbers only 36. Much smaller, older ships might have crews of as many as 60.

Using satellite transmissions, computers continuously pinpoint the ship's location. They keep track of the systems that operate the ship's electricity, plumbing, engines, and automatic steering. They even calculate the best order of filling and emptying the ship's many huge oil tanks. Tanks filled or unloaded in the wrong order might make the ship lean to one side.

Just as planes and ships are changing, so is the automobile. The first automobiles were simply small carriages with motors. Over the years, cars became larger and heavier. Their engines became more powerful. Gasoline was cheap. Three dollars might pay for a fill-up. Most people could easily afford the large amounts of fuel required for big, powerful cars.

Then, in the 1970s, the price of gasoline rose sharply. That caused designers to seek ways to make cars cheaper to operate. One solution: make them smaller.

Designers have also streamlined cars for better performance. At highway speeds, some cars burn more than half their fuel in fighting drag, or air resistance. Many of today's cars have sleek shapes that slice through the wind like sharp knives. They cut gasoline use by as much as 20 percent.

Computers, of course, play a large part in making cars more efficient and, in some cases, easier to repair. Computerized fuel systems, for example, can help increase gas mileage by up to 50 percent. Computers can help spot mechanical and electrical problems. A mechanic just wires a car to a computer that analyzes each system. The computer prints out a complete report of the car's condition. The report notes if anything needs repair.

Carmakers are developing dashboard navigation systems. A computer keeps track of the car's exact location. On a video map, it shows the driver the best route through a city or between one city and another. A Japanese company is experimenting with a car that's equipped with radar. If the car gets too close to a large object, it automatically stops.

Years before automobiles came along, trains were carrying people and freight in many parts of the world. Trains still are a major form of transportation. They haul enormous loads. They are more fuel-efficient than cars, trucks, or airplanes.

The world's two fastest standard trains speed along at about 150 miles an hour (241 km/h). They ride on rails in Japan and in France. Now engineers have developed a new type of train. It can go nearly twice as fast as the fastest trains today. Riders hear only a gentle *shhhhhh*. This train does not ride on rails. Instead, it rides on a cushion of air.

The new trains are called *maglevs*. They work through magnetic levitation, or lifting. Powerful electromagnets[2] raise a maglev train half an inch (one centimeter) above its guideway, or track, and pull it forward. Since no metal-to-metal friction results when it moves, a maglev train can reach much greater speeds than a standard train.

"Riding on a maglev is like flying at ground level," says Paul Sichert, an official with The Budd Company. Budd, located in Troy, Michigan, plans to manufacture maglevs for travel in the United States.

Right now, maglev trains are being built in the Federal Republic of Germany and in Japan. "We expect to see maglevs in operation in the United States by the early 1990s," says Sichert. Maglevs may make it easy to live in one city and work in another hundreds of miles away. A maglev could whisk a worker from Washington, D.C., to New York City, for example, in less than an hour.

"Maglev trains have advantages other than speed alone," says Sichert. "They use energy efficiently. They don't wear out. They have built-in collision safeguards. And they can operate in any kind of weather."

Trains, cars, ships, and planes—they're all changing as we find new ways to travel more rapidly, safely, and conveniently. In the world of transportation, nothing stands still.

---

2. **electromagnets:** pieces of soft iron that become strong magnets when electric currents are passed through coils of wire wrapped around the iron

---

From *Science: It's Changing Your World,* by the National Geographic Society

Unit 3: Chemistry

the science that deals with the study of
substances and the changes they undergo

CRYSTAL, 1947, M.C. Escher, ©1967 M.C. Escher/Cordon Art - Baarn - Holland

What do you notice about what happens to a log when it burns? Do you know why these things happen? For thousands of years people tried to understand fire. Read to find out what discoveries were put together, and when, to finally explain fire.

Patty DiRienzo

What Fire Is

For more than 20,000 years, men struggled to gain mastery over fire without having any clear idea of what fire is. It was only two or three thousand years ago that men began to try to understand fire. They began to look for some way to explain what happened when a piece of wood or other material burst into flame.

Two missing links had to be found before there could be a satisfactory explanation of fire and flame. First, scientists had to discover what there is in air that makes it possible for things to burn. Second, they had to find out more about what goes on inside a substance when it burns.

In the early eighteenth century, a German scientist named Georg Stahl decided that all materials which could be burned contained a certain amount of a substance called *phlogiston*. (Stahl took this word from the Greek word meaning "burnt.") As the material burned, the phlogiston escaped. The phlogiston theory misled scientists for centuries, although it provided a temporary explanation for what appeared to come out of burning substances.

If burning an object used up the phlogiston in it, it might be supposed that the object would weigh less after it was burned. Yet, if a substance is burned, and all the products of its burning—gas, soot, ash, and smoke—are captured and weighed, they will be a little heavier than the original substance.

This problem was solved later in the eighteenth century. In 1774 Joseph Priestley, an English chemist, announced that he had discovered a new gas. A Swedish chemist, Karl Scheele, had already made the same discovery but did not announce his find until later. The great French scientist Antoine Lavoisier—founder of modern chemistry—gave this gas a name. Lavoisier believed that all acids[1] contained some of this gas. He therefore made up a name for it from two Greek words meaning "acid-producing."

The name he decided upon was *oxygen.*

More important than the name was Lavoisier's discovery that oxygen is one of the most valuable and abundant[2] elements of the atmosphere—making up about one-fifth of the air we breathe. Whenever an object burns, it combines chemically with oxygen. And it is the oxygen, added to a burning object, that makes the object weigh more than before it caught fire.

These discoveries supplied the first of the missing links in man's understanding of fire. To supply the second missing link, scientists had to learn some important things about the nature of *matter*—the term used to describe the substances of which everything is composed.

From the time of the ancient Greeks, there had been a theory that all matter is made up of extremely small particles which cannot be divided further. These particles came to be called *atoms,* from the Greek word meaning "cannot be cut" or "indivisible."

In 1808 John Dalton, an English mathematician, paved the way for proof that the atomic theory is basically correct. Dalton also showed that each kind of atom has a size and weight of its own. Atoms can be

---

1. acids: chemical substances that react with other substances in certain predictable ways
2. abundant: in great quantity; plentiful

combined with other atoms to form *molecules* of a substance. A molecule of water, for example, contains one atom of oxygen and two atoms of hydrogen, linked by a *chemical bond*.[3]

Since Dalton's day we have learned a great deal about molecules. We know that, at temperatures normal on earth, these tiny invisible particles that make up all matter are constantly in motion. When you look at a piece of wood or iron or any other substance, you do not see its molecules move. Even when you look at the substance under a powerful microscope, it seems like one solid body. Yet its molecules are moving all the time, like particles of dust in the sunlight.

It is heat that causes molecules to move about. Only at a very low temperature, called absolute zero ($-459°$ F), would they stop moving. Heat, then, is one form of energy.

There is space between the molecules of any substance. The amount of space differs with different substances. There is room for the molecules to move about. At normal temperatures, this is just what they do. When temperatures are raised, molecules move more rapidly; and when temperatures are lowered, they move more slowly.

There are three *states* in which any substance may appear—solid, liquid, or gas. The state depends on the temperature of the substance. Anything on earth will become a solid if you make it cold enough. Nothing on earth can remain a solid if you make it hot enough.

In the case of water, we are familiar with all three states. Below $32°$ F, water is a solid which we call ice. Between $32°$ and $212°$ F, it is a liquid—the water we sail on, swim in, wash and cook with. At temperatures higher than $212°$ F, it is an invisible gas or vapor. (The steam we see coming from a tea kettle is this hot gas becoming water again as it cools on contact with the air.)

As a substance changes from one state to another—for example, from solid to liquid—its molecules begin to behave differently. In a solid, such as ice, the molecules are closest together and move most slowly. In a liquid, such as water, at higher temperature, they move more rapidly. In a vapor, such as steam, which is even hotter, they move most rapidly.

When the temperature of a substance is raised high enough, its molecules may move so rapidly that they can start the molecules of a neighboring substance moving, too. For example, iron may be heated until it glows; if the heated iron is touched to wood, it will stir up the

---

3. **chemical bond:** a holding together due to the tendency of certain atoms to share parts of each other

The flames we see are a lot of tiny explosions that result when elements in the match and the paper combine with oxygen of the air.

molecules of wood. These molecules begin to break down into their separate elements. Some of them combine with the oxygen of the air. When this happens, we have burning, or *combustion*.

When scientists understood this, they had found the second missing link. They now knew what happens to the thing that catches fire. The energy of heat, acting upon the molecules of a substance, causes the molecules to dash about at a great rate of speed. At a high enough temperature, they break down into their separate elements. The breaking of the chemical bond liberates still more energy and thus creates more heat. In this way the elements are freed from their original compound.[4] These combine with the oxygen of the air, resulting in little explosions which are visible as flame. This is fire.

Different substances catch fire at different temperatures. Iron may be hot enough to set fire to wood or paper, though the iron itself does not burst into flame.

The materials which make up the substance we call wood need not be heated to a very high temperature before their restless molecules begin to

---

4. **compound:** substance made up of two or more simpler substances that have been combined chemically

break down. At temperatures of only a few hundred degrees it is easier for them to combine, brilliantly and noisily, with oxygen than to cling quietly to each other and keep the shape and appearance of a log.

Watch a fire from the time it is lighted in a fireplace until it is almost burned out. You will find that there is finally no wood to be seen and no flame, only a heap of gray ashes from which rise tiny wisps of transparent smoke. These ashes occupy very much less space than the logs from which they came. What has happened?

We have said that heat is a form of energy. When the fire dies down, where has that energy gone?

It has, you might say, gone about touching things and leaving a little of itself with everything it has touched. It has touched the stones of the chimney and the air of the room, warming each a little, speeding up the motion of the molecules of the stone and of the air. The energy of the burning wood has spread itself over other things. The molecules of the wood have transferred some of their activity to other objects in the room. Gradually, just as water seeks its level, the heat of the fire has sought its level, too, and has cooled while everything about it has grown warmer. Finally, the molecules of the hearth ash, the chimney stones, the air, and the objects in the room are all moving at such an even rate that they no longer act upon each other.

The energy of the fire's heat has not been lost but merely been scattered over a wide area. Some of it has gone up the chimney and on into the upper air and spread itself there.

From *All about Fire,* by Raymond Holden

The title of this selection describes a substance we all know. What do you think it is? As you read, you'll be suprised to learn some of the ways this substance is used.

All that Glitters,
Spreads, Stretches, and Conducts

It was a clash of gold against gold.

The president's jet came within range, an easy target. Terrorists, hiding out in the mountains below, aimed and launched the heat-seeking missile. The missile's "brain" turned on: electricity flowed through the tiny gold wires of a computer chip. The programmed instructions: seek a point of heat in the sky—the jet's fiery exhaust—and destroy.

The missile sped toward the jet. But military engineers had prepared for this. They'd designed the jet with thin sheets of gold under the wings near the engine. The gold reflected and spread out the heat from the jet's tail. There was no point of heat for the missile to home in on. Luckily, it missed the president by a long shot …

Gold, as you can see, is not just used for mending teeth or making wedding rings.

The gold shielding described in the above spy-novel scenario can be found on United States fighter planes, military helicopters, and the planes used to transport the heads of state of all industrialized countries, according to a spokesperson from the Gold Institute, a gold-industry organization. You can also find gold in VCRs, computers, spacecraft, spark plugs, telephones, and the windows of some buildings.

Why gold? It's virtually indestructible. You can pound it, twist it, and stretch it for miles—and gold will stay together. You can dunk it in most acids or keep it in salt water, and nothing happens. You can send gold through the wash a billion times over and it will still shine, shine, shine.

Animal, Vegetable …

Gold and about 3,000 other substances are minerals. What's a mineral? Well, it's not a vegetable or an animal. In other words, it's not living, nor can it come from things that once lived, the way coal, oil, and natural gas come from once-living plants and animals. Geologists call minerals *inorganic* substances.

A mineral also must occur naturally in the earth. The piece of gold you pan

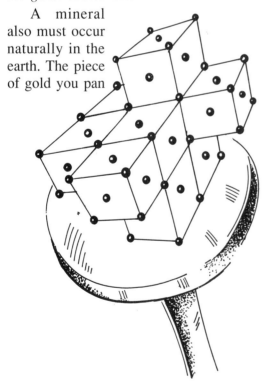

out from mountain streams is a mineral. But the tiny amount of gold physicists make with atom smashers is not.

To be called a mineral, a substance must also have the same chemical makeup wherever you find it. Pure gold is always made of gold atoms, whether it's found in California or South Africa.

Finally, the atoms of a mineral must be packed into a certain geometric shape called a *crystal*.

So a mineral is an inorganic, naturally occurring substance that has a constant chemical makeup and crystal shape.

Sugar Cubes of Gold

Gold's crystal shape is cubic.[1] This shape has a big advantage: it packs 14 atoms—a lot compared to other minerals—into a small space. Think of 14 gold atoms arranged on a sugar cube: one atom on each of the eight corners, and one in the middle of each of the six faces. A gold crystal is made up of many of these sugar cubes, stacked side by side and one on top of the other, like a box of sugar cubes. But the box is much tinier than the head of a pin.

Copper and silver atoms take on the same crystal shape as gold. This is one of the reasons all three minerals have similar properties.

Gold, silver, and copper are *metals*—shiny elements through which electricity can pass. Metals are also *malleable* (able to be hammered into thin sheets) and *ductile* (able to be pulled into thin strands).

---

1. **cubic:** shaped like a cube; having length, breadth, and depth

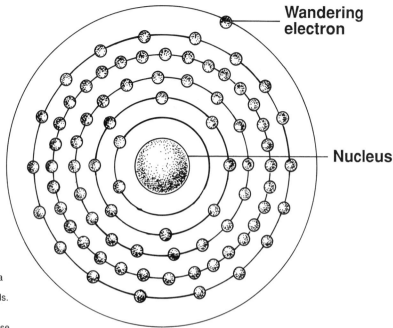

Wandering electron

Nucleus

A gold atom is made up of a nucleus surrounded by 79 electrons in six energy levels. The outermost electron is sometimes called a "wandering" electron because it can join the outer energy level of other gold atoms.

But the structure of the gold atom itself makes gold shine above other metals.

Gold doesn't corrode like iron, the metal used to make steel. Exposed to air or moisture, iron eventually turns to rust. That's because the iron atom readily gives up the electrons[2] in its outer energy level[3] "like someone holding out an ice-cream cone for anyone to take a lick," says chemist William Cooley. Oxygen in the air bonds to iron's outer electrons, and iron oxide, or rust, is formed.

Silver is equally generous with its outer electrons. Eat a poached egg with a silver spoon, says Cooley, and the shiny spoon turns black—it tarnishes. Why? The outer electron in each silver atom bonds to sulfur atoms in the eggs.

Gold—tarnish-proof and rustproof—hoards *all* its electrons, says Cooley. It doesn't want to give up any of the stuff that makes it gold—so it stays gold longer. Even when dug up from ancient Egyptian tombs, gold looks shiny and new.

The shine is more than beautiful. It's useful too. Rust and tarnish block the "free flow" of electrons: electricity. So rustproof gold is used in the communication cables laid across the ocean floor.

For the same reason, there's gold in phone jacks. Carefully unplug a jack and look for little gold-plated contact wires. Though only a few pennies' worth, the gold assures that you hear your friend's voice over the phone without static.

2. **electrons:** in an atom, the parts that have negative electric charge and are outside the nucleus, which is the central part of the atom
3. **outer energy level:** the outermost level at which an electron goes around the nucleus in an atom; atoms can have up to seven energy levels, or shells.

Copper and silver contacts—exposed to the open air—would tarnish and make the voice fuzzy.

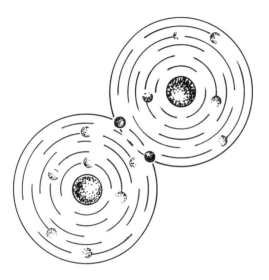

Stretch!

Another amazing trait of gold is its stretchability (its ductility).

Jane Fonda would love it if she could stretch her legs and arms like gold. Imagine if an ounce of gold walked into one of her exercise classes, sat down on the floor, and stretched for 50 miles!

Again, it's gold's electrons that make it so special. In the outermost energy level of every gold atom, there's a lone electron. This electron is far enough away from the pull of its nucleus that it can wander off and visit other gold atoms. The millions of gold atoms in a given gold nugget share these "wandering" electrons, which form a connective "net" around the nugget. When gold is stretched thin, this "net"

holds the gold atoms together—so gold doesn't break. Electrons of brittle metals like tin and iron hold more rigid positions, and so those metals break when stretched.

Technicians can stretch gold into ultrathin wires. Attached to silicon chips, the wires make microscopic electrical networks, much smaller than would be possible with a less stretchy metal. These chips are the brains inside your TV, VCR, computer, calculator—and inside spacecraft and heat-seeking missiles.

Flatter than a Pancake

What do you think would happen if you took a solid ounce of gold and started hammering it? A solid ounce of iron? At a certain point, the iron would break apart. But the gold would hold together in a single sheet 300 feet square. That's because the wandering electrons that give gold its stretchability also give it "squashability"—malleability.

Scientists take advantage of the fact that gold is the most malleable of metals. Thin sheets of shiny gold are excellent reflectors of heat. Firefighters and astronauts wear gold-coated visors to reflect the heat from fires or the sun away from their faces. Spacecraft are also coated with gold, reducing heat buildup to protect sensitive equipment.

French chefs have found a strange use for thin sheets of gold. They decorate pastries with gold leaf. Even stranger, customers gobble them up. Truly we have a taste for gold.

"All that Glitters, Spreads, Stretches, and Conducts," by Jeffrey Brune, from *Science World*

You've probably seen a rusty nail or a rotting log. Did you realize it was an example of chemical change? Read this selection to learn about chemical reactions. Some occur naturally, and some occur because people make them happen.

Chemical Reactions

Change is the keynote of all things, both living and nonliving, from the microscopic ameba[1] to man, from the particles of dust dancing in a beam of sunlight to the proud monument built for the ages. Certain changes, with which we are all familiar, are spectacular and rapid. A blazing fire consumes many square kilometers of forest; a mountain slide sends thousands of metric tons of rocks crashing into the valley below. Other changes are slow and obscure. The restless waves of the ocean gradually carve away the land in one place. In another place, the winds just as gradually deposit many metric tons of dust and create new soil. Nothing escapes change.

All changes, great and small, swift and slow, may be divided into two classes—physical and chemical. A *physical change* does not cause any basic alteration in the molecules of which a given substance is composed. Consider, for instance, what happens when ice melts. The basic particle of ice is a molecule in which two atoms of hydrogen and one of oxygen are held together as a unit. If the ice is allowed to melt so that liquid

---

1. ameba: one-celled organism found in water and moist soils

Ice melting is a physical change. The form of the substance becomes different, but the water molecules remains the same.

Patty DiRienzo

water is formed, the water molecule remains unchanged: it still contains two atoms of hydrogen combined with one of oxygen. It remains unchanged, too, if the liquid water is heated so that it becomes steam. The liquefying of the solid ice and the vaporization of the liquid water are physical changes. They do not alter the composition of the water molecule.

Chemical change is something else again, for it involves the transformation of the molecules of a substance. We saw that only physical changes take place when ice melts or when water turns into steam. But we can bring about a chemical change if we pass a direct electric current through water between two electrodes.[2] The water will gradually disappear, as hydrogen gas forms at one of the electrodes and oxygen gas at the other. In other words, the hydrogen and oxygen atoms that make up the water molecules will break apart and will become molecules of hydrogen and of oxygen.

Nature of Chemical Reactions

Some chemical reactions are produced under natural conditions. Molds and bacteria penetrate a decaying log in a forest and cause the

---

2. electrodes: conductors used to make electrical contact in a circuit

Iron or steel rusting is a chemical change. These metals rust as iron atoms undergo change by joining with atoms of oxygen from the air.

Patty DiRienzo

elements of which it is composed to combine with the oxygen of the air so that in time the log is utterly consumed. Natural chemical reactions also take place when iron rusts, or when peat[3] is formed, or when food is digested in our bodies. Many chemical reactions, however, are deliberately brought about by people under conditions of their own choosing. It is a result of such reactions that coal and petroleum yield synthetic[4] rubber, that the sticky substance called coal tar produces gorgeous dyes, that the stems and stalks of plants give rayon.

Speed of Reactions

Some chemical processes proceed very quickly. In the cylinders of an automobile engine, vaporized gasoline and air (that is, the oxygen in air) react almost instantaneously when fired by an electric spark. Other chemical reactions are very slow. Water, portland cement, and sand, blended together in suitable proportions, react to form concrete, but it takes weeks or months.

The principal factors that influence the speed of a chemical reaction, apart from the very nature of the molecules involved, are (1) the temperature, (2) the degree of contact between the reacting materials,

---

3. peat: heavy soil made of broken-down vegetable matter, used as fertilizer or fuel
4. synthetic: not natural; artificial

(3) the concentration of these materials, and (4) the presence of substances called *catalysts*.

The effect of temperature is an obvious factor. Practically all chemical processes are speeded up by an increase in temperature. All molecules are constantly in motion except at the extreme temperature called absolute zero, corresponding to $-273.16°$ C. As the temperature of a reaction mixture rises, the molecules of reacting substances move with greater speed than before. They collide more often and more vigorously. More and more molecules are jarred so effectively that their atoms are released to form new patterns.

The chemist is generally able to control the temperature at which reactions take place in the laboratory. Sometimes, however, reactions are speeded up by temperature rises that are not due to any human agency. You may have heard of piles of greasy rags, or oily wastes, or fermented straw catching fire of themselves through spontaneous combustion.[5] This is what happens. All these materials undergo oxidation—that is, combination with the oxygen of the air—even under ordinary room temperatures. As a result heat is released. Since the substances in question are poor conductors,[6] they retain a good deal of heat. This raises the temperature, and as the temperature rises oxidation goes on at a more rapid rate. At last combustible gases are expelled, and by this time the temperature is so high that the materials burst into flame.

The degree of contact between reacting molecules also influences greatly the speed of reaction. The grinding up of large solid particles into very fine ones speeds up a reaction because it causes contact over a vastly increased area. Let us take the fuel coal as an example. Coal burns because the carbon of the coal reacts vigorously with the oxygen of the air at a high temperature. It takes time to set fire to large chunks of coal, because the amount of surface that is exposed to oxygen is limited. But powdered coal offers an almost infinite number of points of contact. If such fuel is blown out of a nozzle, so that the particles will not pack together, it burns almost as rapidly as liquid fuel.

It is because particles of coal dust, sawdust, and grain dust are so finely divided that dust is an ever-present danger in coal mines, sawmill factories, and grain elevators. The total surface exposed to the oxygen of the air is so great that a mere spark may cause a terrible explosion. Even

---

5. **spontaneous combustion:** a bursting into flame without heat from an outside source
6. **conductors:** transmitters or relayers, in this case, of heat

In which form of coal pictured above is more surface area in contact with the oxygen of the air? Which will burn more quickly?

aluminum and bronze dust will be ignited and burn up at an explosive rate under such conditions.

Catalysts

Even when the temperature is high and when reacting substances are in intimate contact, some reactions will take place slowly. In such cases outside materials, not involved in the reaction, will sometimes speed up the chemical change. These outside materials are called catalysts. They are generally solids, but they may be liquids or gases. They modify the rate of a reaction without themselves undergoing any permanent change. Different catalysts are used to modify the rate of different reactions. Living cells contain natural catalysts, called enzymes, which make possible many of the chemical changes occurring within the cells.

The chemist makes frequent use of catalysts. Sometimes he adds them in small quantities to reacting materials. Thus he combines finely divided nickel with cottonseed oil so that the oil will react with hydrogen gas to form the solid fats sold as shortening or used in the manufacture of soap. In other cases, the catalyst is present in a bed over which the reacting materials are passed.

"Chemical Reactions," by Hilton A. Smith, from *The New Book of Popular Science*

Have you ever had to buy paint? How did you decide what kind you needed? Whether you're a do-it-yourself sort of person or not, you'll be surprised at what there is to learn about paint. Read this selection, and the next time you or someone you know begins a paint job, this information will come in handy.

What Makes Paint Stick

One of the most famous paintings of Western civilization, *The Last Supper* by Italian genius Leonardo da Vinci, began to flake away soon after he completed the work in about 1497. This wall painting was a triumph of art, but a failure of surface chemistry.

Today, anybody who merely wants to cover an interior or exterior wall with paint can easily outclass Leonardo when it comes to making paint stick. Modern chemistry has developed paints that look good, do an excellent job of protecting the surfaces they cover, and are extremely durable.[1]

But with so many paints available today, how do we know which paint is best for a given job? The best advice is to discuss the job with a reliable paint dealer. A little knowledge of paint chemistry and surface preparation can help you talk the dealer's language.

Paints are made up of three kinds of materials—pigments, binders, and liquids. *Pigments* are solid particles that give paints their color. *Binders,* which include plastics and resins,[2] make paints dry to a filmy consistency, hold the pigments to the surface, and protect the surface. *Liquids* give paints their fluid form, making them easy to apply. The liquid is also known as the *base,* and there are two main types of base—oil and water.

To protect and beautify a surface effectively, a paint must have certain properties. It must be easy to apply smoothly and evenly. It must stick to the surface, forming a single, unbroken film of uniform thickness.

For safety's sake, the paint should not be highly poisonous or flammable.[3] For convenience, it should dry quickly, be easy to clean up, and last a long time in storage.

Once the paint is dry, it should resist chemicals, water, and sunlight. Interior

---

1. durable: lasting a long time; able to withstand wear
2. resins: sticky yellow or brownish substances that come from certain plants
3. flammable: easily set on fire

paints must resist cleaning solvents, while exterior paints have to contend with weather.

In addition, the paint should be simple to touch up, easy to wipe clean, and strong and flexible enough to resist dents and scratches. The color should resist fading.

No paint excels in all these ways, however. So you must find a paint that has the best balance of properties for the job you want it to do.

Paints bind to surfaces in two basic ways—mechanically and chemically. In *mechanical binding,* the paint locks itself to the surface by filling in tiny holes and uneven areas in the surface. In *chemical binding,* atoms in the paint form bonds with surface atoms so that the paint and the surface become one continuous material. Thus, chemical binding forms a smoother surface than does mechanical binding.

Two critical properties of paints— strength and stability—depend on what happens to the molecules that make up the binders. When oil-based paints dry, molecules of their binders join to form surface films that are tougher and more stable than are those of water-based paints. The way in which the long, chainlike molecules of the binders join is called *cross-linking.* When the paint dries, chemical bonds form between the chains, resulting in netlike structures that are extremely tough. This makes oil-based paint best for most outdoor surfaces.

Oil-based paints are brittle when they dry, however, and they crack easily. Other disadvantages of oil-based paints include the need to use thinning and cleaning solvents such as turpentine that may have strong-smelling, flammable, even toxic fumes.

Oil-based paints also tend to deteriorate quickly in storage. The binders in the unused paint, over time, may begin to cross-link in the can, forming a thick "skin" and eventually drying up altogether. To combat these problems, paint chemists have developed additives that limit cross-linking, reduce the amount of solvent required, and cut the rate of drying in the can.

Most water-based paints form a hard surface by *solvent evaporation.* The water dries and the binders stick to one another mechanically. The resulting films on surfaces are not as strong as those of oil-based paints.

Water-based paints are chemically stable, however, and their fumes are not poisonous or flammable. In addition, spills and paint-coated brushes are easy to clean up. This makes water-based paints good for interior walls.

Older water-based paints, such as whitewashes and lacquers, did not hold up well over time and were difficult to apply. Newer latex[4] paints go a long way toward solving these problems. Their binders are plastics whose molecules overlap one another as they dry, forming tough, netlike structures. The addition of *surfactants*—soaplike molecules that reduce the surface tension of the paint—makes latex paint spread more evenly.

One problem with latex paints is that microorganisms reproduce easily in

---

4. **latex:** synthetic rubber or plastic combined with water

Preparing Surfaces and Choosing the Right Paint

Outdoor Surfaces

Type of Surface	Preparation	Paint
New wood	Use primer to seal. Putty or caulk nailheads, cracks, and areas around windows. Use knot sealer to prevent resin in knots from staining paint.	Latex, oil-based, or *alkyd*-based paint (an alkyd is an artificial chemical base); stain; or varnish
Previously painted wood	Remove chipped, blistered, or powdered paint by scraping. Remove unusually stubborn old paint by such means as a chemical stripper. Replace loose or shrunken putty and caulk. Prime bare areas.	Latex, oil-based, or alkyd-based paint
Wood deck or stairs	Prime with paintable water-repellent preservative.	Porch and deck enamel
Aluminum gutters	Remove dirt and cracking and flaking paint. Prime bare areas with primer manufactured for aluminum or galvanized steel.	Metal enamel or any paint suitable for exterior wood.
Cement block	Fill large holes with cement grout. For a top coat of masonry paint, prime with masonry surface conditioner. For other top coats, prime with alkali-resistant paint. (Any alkali is a substance such as lime that can destroy paint films.)	Exterior latex paint

them before the paint is used, making the paint turn sour. Paint chemists have minimized souring by adding antibacterial and antifungal chemicals to the paints.

Another problem with latex paints is the difficulty in getting a glossy finish. Gloss depends upon smoothness. The smoother the film, the glossier the finish. And smoothness depends on how the paint sticks to the surface.

Because water-based paints tend to bind more mechanically than chemically, they do not form as smooth a film as do chemical bonds and so it is difficult to

get a glossy surface with a latex paint. Acrylic binders in modern water-based paints, however, form such strong chemical bonds with surface atoms that they dry to a gloss approaching that of oil-based paints.

The surface plays as important a role in the sticking process as the paint. The best paint in the world cannot do the job unless the surface is prepared to accept it.

The surface must be very clean. Even greasy fingerprints can prevent a paint from sticking well.

The surface must be smooth. Paint can hide slight imperfections, but not

Indoor Surfaces

Type of Surface	Preparation	Paint
Woodwork	For a top coat of paint on new wood, first cover with a primer. For paint on previously painted wood, remove any peeling and cracked paint, then sand. For a top coat of stain on open-grained woods such as oak, undercoat with paste wood filler. Close-grain woods such as maple do not need a filler.	Latex, or alkyd-based flat, semigloss, or high-gloss paint; stain; varnish; or polyurethane varnish
Wooden floors	Sand off any old finish. For a top coat of floor enamel, apply wood filler, then prime with same paint as top coat. For a top coat of sealer, varnish, or lacquer, undercoat with wood filler to fill the pores of the wood, providing a smooth finish.	Floor enamel; floor sealer; varnish; clear floor lacquer; or polyurethane varnish
Previously painted plaster and drywall	Scrub off grease and dirt.	Latex or alkyd-based semigloss or gloss enamel paint for heavy-use areas such as kitchens and bathrooms; latex or alkyd-based flat paint or semigloss enamel paint for moderate-use areas such as halls and children's rooms; latex or alkyd-based flat paint for light-use areas such as living rooms and bedrooms
New plaster	Wait three or four weeks after plaster is applied before priming.	
New drywall	Sand joint compound lightly to provide an even finish, then cover with latex prime coat.	

bumps or pits. The surface should not be glossy, however. Paint needs some roughness to latch onto, particularly if the paint relies heavily on mechanical binding. A *primer* (undercoat) can roughen a surface and improve mechanical binding.

The surface and the paint must suit each other chemically. A surface that absorbs liquids extremely well, for example, must be sealed with a primer or a thin liquid called a *sealer* to prevent the paint from soaking in too far. A sealer dries to form a film that paints cannot soak through.

A surface, such as a plastic, that can be damaged by a paint's chemical solvents also must be protected with a primer. If the paint relies on the formation of chemical bonds for adhesion,[5] the surface must contain the types of atoms that can form those bonds. If the surface does not contain such atoms, you must put them on the

---

5. adhesion: sticking

surface by coating it with a primer. Metal surfaces, for example, do not form strong chemical bonds with many exterior paints, so they require a coat of a special primer made for metals.

If you are using an oil-based paint, the surface must be dry, because oil and water do not mix. Water is an enemy of oil-based paint and can cause blistering and bleeding.

To prepare a surface properly, follow these six steps:

1. Examine the surface closely and diagnose any problems. If there are several layers of old paint, the new paint's resistance to temperature changes will be reduced, so you should remove the old paint. If a panel of wood has rotted, replace it.

2. If old paint is blistered or peeling, remove it by scraping, by heating and scraping, or by applying a chemical paint remover. If paint is severely blistered, you may have a moisture problem. Water vapor may be leaking through the wall. The only way to solve this problem is to install a moisture barrier—usually a sheet of thin plastic—in the wall.

3. Clean the surface thoroughly. Follow rinsing instructions on the cleanser label to remove harmful residues.[6]

4. Fill small cracks and holes with a caulking compound,[7] joint compound,[8] plaster, putty, or plastic wood. Then sand the excess filler, bumps, and other irregularities. When you are finished with your repair work, the surface should feel smooth to the touch, but not slick.

5. Clean the surface again to remove all dust generated by the repair work.

6. Add a coat of primer or sealer, if appropriate.

The same chemicals that provide a paint with desirable qualities such as a smooth, durable surface and fast drying may also be dangerous, so a few simple precautions are necessary:

• Work with adequate ventilation.[9]

• Avoid open flames such as burning cigarettes and gas pilot lights when using turpentine and other flammable solvents for oil-based paints.

• Close the containers of flammable liquids tightly and, when finished, store them carefully.

• Dispose of solvent-soaked rags as you finish with them. Heaps of such rags are a fire hazard because they can burst into flame spontaneously.[10]

• Wear gloves and other protective clothing to protect your skin.

• Read all product labels and follow manufacturers' instructions.

Now you should be ready to talk with your dealer about what kind of paint to use. Then—move over, Leonardo.

---

6. **residues:** substances that are left behind
7. **caulking compound:** substance used to fill seams and cracks so they will not leak
8. **joint compound:** substance like caulking compound used to prevent leaks in places where parts come together
9. **ventilation:** flow of air
10. **spontaneously:** by themselves; in this case, without heat from an outside source

---

"What Makes Paint Stick," by Peter J. Andrews, from *Science Year, The 1989 World Book Annual Science Supplement*

Unit 4: Earth Science

the science that deals with the study of the earth or one or more of its parts

THE CREATION OF THE EARTH, 1990, Gerald N. Bates, mixed media on board, private collection.

What are some of the reasons people need water? Water covers nearly three-fourths of the earth's surface. We could not live without it. Read this selection to find out how water came to exist on earth.

UPI/Bettmann Archives

Water–
the Essence of Life

Of all the earth's resources, water is the most precious. Without it no plant or animal could have evolved.

Where did the water come from that makes life possible? The most widely accepted theory proposes that water in the form of vapor was one of the compounds present in very small amounts in the vast gaseous[1] cloud of hydrogen and helium from which our sun evolved. The sun became a separate body without using up all the matter in the cosmic cloud. What remained whirled through space and after millions of years

---

1. **gaseous:** in the form of gases; not liquid or solid

became the nine planets of our solar system. The water from the original cloud, according to this theory, became a part of each planet, but was not necessarily evenly distributed. The amount of water present and the form it took—solid, liquid, or vapor—depended on the planet's mass and its distance from the sun.

Through the happiest of accidents, the earth is the right size and distance from the sun to permit water to exist in all three forms. It is in its liquid form that water is essential to the life process. And it is in liquid form that water is rare in the universe. Close to the sun the heat is so intense that water is vaporized. Far from the sun it is so cold that water remains permanently frozen. Of the other planets, only Mars, our second nearest neighbor, is in the narrow temperature band in which water can exist in its three forms. Thus, extraterrestrial[2] life in our solar system is deemed possible only on Mars. Whether life, in fact, exists on Mars we do not yet know.

Every drop of water on earth when earth was formed remains on our planet today. It has since gone many times around the globe; water is constantly moving. It is pulled from the oceans by the heat of the sun and moved along in clouds by winds. It may fall from the sky as rain, snow, sleet, or hail. It may fall in any latitude[3] from Arctic to Antarctic. It will stay for ages in icecaps and glaciers, or return promptly to the sea through storm sewers and rivers. Almost all of the water on earth today is in the oceans. Life itself is thought to have begun there. No one is sure exactly how. But at an unknown time, probably about three billion years ago, some fortuitous[4] circumstance made it possible for chemical substances dissolved in the warm broth of the sea to combine with each other to form molecules with the unique ability of reproducing themselves. From those first living molecules all life has descended.

Water Is Precious

Water, along with sunlight and oxygen, is one of the prime ingredients that make life on earth possible. Without water, life as we know it just can't be. So water is one of our most precious assets. Deserts are virtually waterless and virtually lifeless too. Oceans, on the other hand, are virtually all water, and the oceans teem with life.

---

2. **extraterrestrial:** outside the planet earth and its atmosphere
3. **latitude:** distance north or south of the equator, the center ring around the globe
4. **fortuitous:** lucky

From *The Ocean World of Jacques Cousteau: Oasis in Space,* by Jacques Cousteau

On a hot, sticky day, you might have said the words that are the title of this selection. How does humidity affect you? Do you know exactly what it is? This selection may surprise you with the effects humidity has on us and things around us.

It's Not the Heat,
It's the Humidity

When the weather in the Midwest turns humid, some prize dairy Holsteins produce less milk and conceive fewer offspring.

In the South, summers are so humid, according to local wags,[1] you'll see a hound dog chasing a jack rabbit and both will be walking.

And during steamy days in Washington, D.C., before short-sleeved shirts were finally issued as part of their uniforms, some members of the U.S. Army National Honor Guard cut the backs and sleeves off their starched white shirts and pinned false cuffs to their dress-blue jackets. The men stayed cool, looked sharp, and no one was the wiser.

What is this sultry thing that's all around us, wreaking havoc, affecting our bodies, our minds, even our pocketbooks? The answer, of course, is *humidity*—which is simply a measure of the amount of water in the air. Relative humidity, the term most commonly used to describe atmospheric moisture, compares actual water vapor with the amount of water the air can absorb at a particular temperature. The warmer the

---

1. **wags:** witty or joking persons

air, the more water it can hold—90° air can soak up almost twice as much water as 70° air can.

The oceans are the main source of humidity, but plants also pour moisture into the air. In one day, a five-acre forest can release 20,000 gallons of water, enough to fill an average swimming pool. A dryer extracts moisture from wet clothes, adding to humidity. Even breathing contributes to this sticky business. Every time we exhale, we expel nearly one pint of moist air into the atmosphere.

Using sophisticated measuring devices, science is learning more and more about the far-reaching and often surprising impact humidity has on all of us.

Two summers ago angry callers phoned American Television and Communications Corp.'s cable-TV operation in northeastern Wisconsin, complaining about fuzzy pictures and poor reception. "What happened," said the chief engineer, "was that the humidity was interfering with our signals." When a blast of dry air invaded the state, the number of complaints dropped sharply.

Humidity plays hob with our mechanical world as well. Water condensation on the playing heads and tapes of videocassette recorders produces a streaky picture. Humidity shortens the life of flashlight and smoke-detector batteries. When the weather gets sticky, the rubber belts that power the fan, air conditioner, and alternator under the hood of our cars can get wet and squeak.

Moisture also causes pianos to go out of tune, often in no time flat. At the Wolf Trap Farm Park for the Performing Arts in Vienna, Virginia, pianos are tuned twice a day during the summer concert season. Often a tuner stands in the wings, ready to make emergency adjustments during performances.

Humidity speeds the deterioration of treasured family photos and warps priceless antiques. Your home's wooden support beams, doors, and window frames absorb extra moisture and expand—swelling up to three percent depending on the wood, its grain, and the setting.

Too much moisture promotes blight[2] that attacks potato and green bean crops—adding to food costs. It also causes rust[3] in wheat, which can affect grain-product prices.

A recent five-state survey of nearly 1,500 employees in 11 major industries showed that on-the-job accidents increased 33 percent when humidity levels reached 80 percent or higher. In a Chicago study, stenographic errors increased 1,000 percent when temperature and humidity rose.

Research shows that 90-percent relative humidity makes a pleasant summer temperature of 80° feel like an 88° heat wave. Dry air absorbs sweat as fast as the body's several million sweat glands produce it, keeping us cool. Humid air—already saturated with moisture—can't absorb sweat. Perspiration builds up on the skin,

---

2. **blight:** plant disease that causes leaves, stems, and fruits to wither and die
3. **rust:** plant disease that spots leaves and stems

body temperature goes up, and we're miserable.

Humidity affects our health, as well. We get more migraine headaches, ulcer attacks, blood clots, and skin rashes in hot, humid weather. Since 1987, the Health, Weight, and Stress Clinic at John Hopkins Hospital in Baltimore has tested over 1,700 patients for responses to high humidity. They have reported increased dizziness, stomachaches, chest pains, cramps, and visual disturbances such as double and blurred vision.

As humidity soars, urban violence seems to rise. Natural deaths go up. Wife abuse increases; sexual activity may decrease.

Appearances wither too. Oily skin breaks out. Human hair absorbs enough extra moisture to stretch nearly 2.5 percent in length, making curly hair frizz and straight hair wilt. "Humidity makes me feel like an unmade bed," a beauty-salon patron wailed during one of Atlanta's sticky spells.

Adding insult to injury, humidity even makes us look fatter. "When the relative humidity rises," says Maria Simonson of Baltimore's Health, Weight, and Stress Clinic, "the body takes up more water from the intestinal tract. This causes swelling that can add an inch to the waistline and legs."

But the news about humidity is not all bad. Highly humidified air can be a lifesaver for people suffering from pneumonia, bronchial infections, and other lung-related conditions. And contact lenses are more comfortable in humid weather.

Still, there is something relentless about the days when summer seems to simmer. For those without air conditioning or fans, here are some good ways to beat the heat:

- If you can stand the thought, G. Edgar Folk, Jr., professor of physiology at the University of Iowa, advocates taking a hot shower. At the very least, he advises, keep the water warm. Warm water makes you sweat more, but that's good, Folk says. By increasing blood volume and dilating[4] blood vessels in your system, you're acclimating[5] your body to the weather.

- Eat less, because metabolism[6] raises body heat. And drink lots of water. But avoid too many caffeinated beverages. Caffeine is a diuretic that promotes urine flow and dries out the body. Cut down on alcoholic and highly sugared drinks too. Alcohol dehydrates[7] the body, and sugar delays water absorption.

- Dress appropriately. Loose cotton clothing increases air flow, drawing moisture from the surface and keeping your body temperature down.

Sometimes, of course, there's just simply no dealing with humidity. Energy dwindles and the most stringent resolve melts. When this happens, blame the weatherman. He's used to it.

---

4. **dilating:** making larger or wider
5. **acclimating:** getting used to new conditions
6. **metabolism:** the set of processes, including changing food into energy, by which an organism maintains life
7. **dehydrates:** takes the water out of

"It's Not the Heat, It's the Humidity," by Patricia Skalka, from *Reader's Digest*

Do you think of snow as being light and fluffy? It may be hard to believe, but a six-inch snowfall on an acre of land weighs 113 tons. Imagine how many snowflakes that takes! In this selection, you'll learn some fun and amazing facts about what the Greeks called "woolly water."

Tony Stone Worldwide

Snow
in Every Shape and Form

Eskimos have about 70 words for snow, which is not surprising. No doubt they would be amazed to know that we have a similarly large number of words for grass—rye, Bermuda, dichondra, crab, etc. But the Eskimos are to grass as we are to snow: largely unaware of its many forms and varieties, its secrets and mysteries.

The Eskimos of Greenland, for example, distinguish between snow that is falling, *ganik,* and snow that has fallen, *aput.* Canadian Eskimos go further in denoting the subtleties: they have a dozen words that describe snow according to its degree of fineness or coarseness and softness or hardness—

conditions that affect the running of their sleds.

By contrast, according to "The Wonder of Snow" by Corydon Bell, the ancient Greek words for snow literally meant "woolly water" and "wet wool." The Greeks seemed to regard snow more as a nuisance than as a benefactor.

And yet we of warmer climes are no less dependent on snow than our Eskimo brethren. Because of a single cosmic quirk, the tilting of earth on its axis, we pass through seasonal fluctuations,[1] including winter and its snow. Although we sometimes curse snow for the

---

1. fluctuations: changes

| Plate | Stellar Crystal | Column |

The seven basic types of snow crystals

inconvenience it causes, without it and the water it provides, life on earth would not be as we know it.

How much does a single snowflake weigh? Almost nothing, really. Yet a six-inch layer of wet new snow over an acre of land weighs 113 tons. That's a lot of "almost nothing." It's no wonder that roofs in snow country are angled, not flat. A 10-inch snowfall on a flat roof measuring 100 by 150 feet weighs 39 tons. In the same snowfall, a small house of 40 by 75 feet would be supporting almost nine tons, Bell says.

Then consider: if New York state were uniformly covered by a 15-inch fall, the snow could weigh more than 5 billion tons.

The "permanent snow" of glaciers and icecaps covers 12 percent of earth's land surface. If it were possible to carve up the Greenland icecap into jumbo-sized ice cubes, every man, woman, and child would have a new two-ton chunk available every minute of the year.

And the Greenland ice sheet accounts for only 10 percent of earth's ice mass. Antarctica represents 85 percent of the ice crust, and the remaining five percent is in the form of glaciers scattered over the world's high mountains.

A fair number of those mountains are found in equatorial[2] regions—Mt.

Kilamanjaro and Mt. Kenya in Africa, for example.

If all of the world's ice were to melt (an increasingly ominous[3] possibility, given earth's accelerating[4] rate of warming), sea levels would rise by 200 feet. Continental shores would recede, ports would disappear, the very shape of landforms would change.

Most people think of snowflakes as those lovely six-pointed or six-sided configurations that illustrate Christmas cards. But those are snow crystals, not snowflakes, which actually are large bunches of crystals.

Nor is every snow crystal a thing of beauty. In fact, most are unimpressive clumps of ice—irregular, asymmetric,[5] and modified (injured, really) by collisions with other snow particles, by wind or by rime (a deposit of frozen water particles on the surface of the crystal).

Nevertheless, there is an astonishing variety among snow crystals. They have been classified into seven types, within which are 37 variations that are regularly discoverable in snowfalls. Within these is an apparently limitless number of

2. **equatorial:** near the equator, the center ring around the planet
3. **ominous:** representing future disaster
4. **accelerating:** faster
5. **asymmetric:** not looking the same on each side of an imaginary line through the center

| Needle | Spatial Dendrite | Capped Column | Irregular Crystal |

crystalline forms, some of which are exquisitely symmetrical[6] and complex. Rarely, in fact, does a crystal formation show the same intricate pattern on both front and back.

Although snow crystals were studied in China as early as the second century B.C., when their six-sided nature was noted, German astronomer and mathematician Johannes Kepler in the seventeenth century was the first Westerner to take a scientific interest in their patterns and forms.

One winter morning after a night spent observing the stars, Kepler stepped out of the observatory at Prague and suddenly became aware of other stars, tiny ones, that shone brightly on the dark fur that edged his thick coat. Although the crystals were of myriad[7] design, all of their branching forms seemed to fall into one definite pattern.

In 1611 Kepler wrote, as a New Year's gift to his benefactor,[8] a short, lively essay in which he tried to answer the question: "why snowflakes in their falling, before they are entangled in larger plumes, always fall with six corners and with six rods, tufted like feathers?"

Kepler was not aware that many snow crystals have nonhexagonal[9] shapes, but he did raise an interesting point: why indeed? His fascinating, witty essay draws up much that was interesting at the time in both science and religion without, however, succeeding in answering the question (which, by the way, remained un-answered until an understanding of atomic particles provided at least a partial explanation).

Eventually Kepler had to fall back on the concept of the universal spirit pervading and shaping everything. But this inquiry was the beginning of what turned into a growth market in the investigation of snow and snow crystals. Since Kepler's time, scientists have studied every aspect of snow, and their research has had widespread applications in agriculture, mining, and transportation. Their work has allowed hydrologists,[10] for example, to predict snowpack runoff[11] based on the climatic conditions affecting snowfall, an application of major importance to agriculture.

---

6. **symmetrical:** looking the same on two sides of an imaginary line through the center
7. **myriad:** many; countless
8. **benefactor:** person who helps another with money or some other means
9. **nonhexagonal:** not having six sides or points
10. **hydrologists:** scientists who study water
11. **snowpack runoff:** water that runs off of a field of packed snow as it slowly melts during the early summer months

---

"Snow in Every Shape and Form," by Robert Speer, from the *Chicago Tribune*

What is your reaction to the sea? Are you frightened by it? Are you attracted to it or curious about it? As you read this selection, you will learn how people have studied the sea and how we all depend on the products of the sea.

The Sea

The sea long kept its secrets locked deep in its mysterious depths. For centuries, people's interest in the sea was chiefly concerned with obtaining food from its shorelines and sailing their fragile crafts on its waters. Not until the middle of the nineteenth century did people undertake serious study of that strange world beneath the surface of the sea.

The sea scientists (who came to be known as oceanographers) were first interested in learning things about the sea that would aid shipping. Ship captains needed to know more about the great ocean currents. In what direction did the currents flow? How fast did they flow? For greater safety, mariners needed more information about the sea bottom, especially near the land.

As the study of the sea progressed, exploratory cruises were made to various parts of the world by the ships of many nations. The oceanographers began hunting the answers to such questions as: How deep is the sea? What is the ocean floor like? How salty is the sea? How hot or cold are its waters? What chemicals occur in sea water? Is there life in the lower levels?

Unlocking the Secrets of the Sea

How the Sea Was Studied

Answering these questions was a tremendous task, for the oceans cover nearly three-fourths of the earth's surface. At first the oceanographers had few instruments with which to work. Thus, special instruments had to be devised to help them "look" into that little-known world. With sounding line[1] and later with echo-sounders[2] and sonar, which sends back electronic echoes revealing the distance to the ocean floor, they began mapping the depths of the sea; with nets towed behind the vessel they collected many forms of sea life—from tiny animals and plants that make up plankton[3] to large fishes and squids. Water bottles were lowered over the side to collect animals and plants and water samples that would reveal the salinity (saltiness) of the sea water. In recent years, the bathythermograph,[4] lowered by wire from the deck of a

1. **sounding line:** line or wire used to determine the depth of a body of water
2. **echo-sounders:** instruments that measure the depth of a body of water (or of an object in the water) by means of sound waves that bounce off the floor (or off the object)
3. **plankton:** mass of tiny sea animals and plants that drifts at or near the surface of the sea
4. **bathythermograph:** instrument that measures the temperatures of a body of water at different depths

ship, has enabled sea scientists to measure the temperatures of the sea from the surface to hundreds of feet deep, under burning tropical suns and in cold, foggy polar regions.

While such routine surveys of the sea are continuing in many distant parts of the world, oceanographers for many years have studied the seas more analytically.[5] By the end of the nineteenth century they began to realize that the sea is a living thing, that forces keep it continually in motion. Their inquiries led them to study, among other things, the forces producing the ocean currents; the causes underlying the spectacular migration of sea animals; the marked fluctuations in the size of fish populations; and the intricate relation between a sea animal and its environment.

The recently invented bathyscaph[6] lets people descend six miles into the sea to study and photograph animals and plants living in the depths. Underwater television enables people to study the sea and its inhabitants' behavior from the safety of the ship's laboratories. Electronic devices reveal the presence of fish; underwater cameras, operated from shipboard or triggered when the equipment touches bottom, take pictures of the ocean floor.

What the Oceanographers Discovered

The oceanographers learned many things. They learned that all the continents are surrounded by gently sloping platforms of varying widths, the Continental Shelves; descending abruptly from the shelves are the Continental Slopes; the slopes end in the great ocean basins. They learned the bottom of the sea is not a level plain, but that mountains and valleys exist in this submarine world. The largest mountain range in the sea is in the Atlantic Ocean—its tallest peak, 27,000 feet high, forms an island in the Azores. They discovered great depressions, or trenches, in the sea floor—probably the deepest one is the Mindanao Trench off the Philippines, with its bottom about 6 1/2 miles below the sea surface. They found that great rivers cut through the sea, such as the subsurface Cromwell Current in the central equatorial Pacific, and that sea life is most abundant where there is a rapid exchange of nutrient-rich waters—as where great ocean currents come together or great tidal currents sweep certain coasts.

---

5. analytically: by using logical reasoning, or by looking at the separate parts that make up a thing
6. bathyscaph: a ship that can withstand the high water pressure and be used in deep-sea exploration

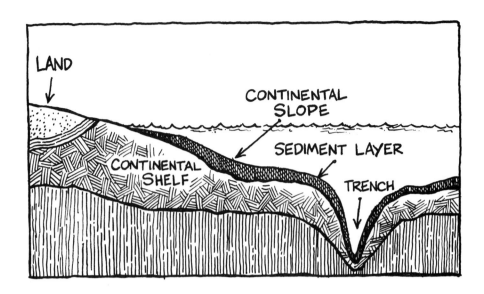

They learned that the floor of the Pacific is underlaid with basalt,[7] while in other oceans it is granite;[8] that the oceans vary in their salinity—the Atlantic being the most saline and the polar seas, because of melting ice and snow, the least salty; and that sea temperatures range from 28° F in the northern seas to 96° F in the Persian Gulf. They found that great currents sweep from ocean basin to ocean basin, driven by the winds and urged on by the force of the earth's rotation. They learned that sea life does exist in the great ocean basins, which cover more than half of the earth's surface, and that in these eerie depths animal preys on animal, for plants cannot live below 600 feet. From this forbidding, darkened world come fish with great eyes to take advantage of the faintest light; fish with luminous spots on their sides or heads; squid that expel shining clouds instead of the "ink" of their relatives of the upper layers; and at still deeper depths, where eyes are no longer useful, sensitive feelers or lengthened fins help the blind fish find food.

Practical Value of Sea Studies

How do people benefit by studying the sea? The benefits are many, but we will consider principally the living resources. The sea is a vast natural farm. It can produce great quantities of nutritious protein food forever if we manage this farm wisely. We need to know how much we can harvest from the sea each year; yet we also must leave enough behind

---

7. basalt: hard, dark-colored rock that came from the action of volcanoes
8. granite: hard rock with crystal-like texture that came from the action of volcanoes

to ensure the next year's crop. Scientists know how to obtain the information they need. But it is difficult and expensive to get accurate and sufficient information.

The next step will be to learn how to apply our scientific knowledge to increase the yield of food from the sea. Then we may be able to farm the sea scientifically, just as our farmers on land now lead the world in agricultural production. This is the goal that fishery scientists hope to reach.

Other uses, also, are made of the work of sea scientists. Through their study of ocean currents and drift and the mapping of ocean floors, they have contributed greatly to the safety of shipping. Charting of undersea mountain ranges and trenches are vital information for the submarine navigator and those laying undersea cables. Meteorologists need to know about the wind patterns at sea and about sea surface temperatures to predict ocean swells[9] and weather accurately.

Products of the Sea

Living Resources

When we speak of things that come from the sea, most of us probably think first of its fish and shellfish, such as cod, herring, halibut, tuna, oysters, crabs, scallops, lobsters, and clams.

Fish are the main source of protein—an important body builder—for many people of the world, notably the Japanese. The average American uses only about one-seventh the fish consumed by the average Japanese. Fish are an economical way to obtain one's supply of protein. It comes as a surprise to most of us to learn that the amount of protein in an average serving of fish is equal to, and often higher than, that in an average serving of beef. Fish and shellfish also supply valuable vitamins.

You probably are wondering how these important nutrients came to be in the fish and shellfish. Doubtless you have heard of the "food chain." You know that it means the passing of nutrients from one animal or plant to another, the chain progressing from the simplest to the most complex organisms. These nutrients—elements, minerals, and organic compounds, such as carbon, oxygen, nitrogen, phosphorus, chlorine, iodine, boron, magnesium, calcium, silicon, as well as proteins and carbohydrates—have been recycling in the sea for many eons. Billions of

---

9. swells: long, often large, waves that may result from a storm

minute,[10] floating sea animals and plants (plankton) use these nutrients to build their bodies. Juvenile[11] fish, plankton-feeding fish such as the menhaden and herrings, crustaceans, and many other sea animals live on plankton. These animals, in turn, are fed on by such larger carnivores[12] as tunas, halibuts, sharks, and squids. When sea animals die, the nutrients return to the sea to be used by succeeding generations. When you eat fish and shellfish, you, too, take these nutrients into your body.

Another valuable living resource the sea has given us is our marine mammals.[13] The sea otter and fur seal, highly regarded for their valuable furs; the gray whale and sea elephant, once nearly destroyed for their oil; the walrus, whose tusks provide ivory for the Aleut carvers of Alaska; and the California sea lion, whose trained antics have entertained generations of Americans at the circus and in zoo pools, all live along our Pacific coast.

The seaweeds along our seacoasts are among the sea's most valuable living resources. Americans make little use of them in their natural state, but Japanese cooks prepare many tasty dishes from them. The greatest value of seaweeds in America comes from the chemical and industrial products derived from them. The derivatives, algin, agar, and carrageenin, are used in many ways: in foods, such as ice cream, candies, and cake icings; in drugs, such as aspirin, antacid tablets, and calamine lotions; in manufacturing processes producing rubber, textiles, acoustic[14] tiles, and numerous other commercial items. A valuable derivative of seaweeds, mannitol, is used in explosives and medicinal drugs.

If our valuable living resources of the sea are to be preserved we must look well at the way we treat our seacoasts. Along these coasts, over the Continental Shelves, are found the world's most valuable

---

10. **minute:** very small; tiny
11. **juvenile:** young; not yet adult
12. **carnivores:** meat-eaters
13. **mammals:** animals with backbones and hair that feed their young with milk
14. **acoustic:** absorbing sound and, thus, reducing the noise level

fisheries. Here are the shellfish-producing areas and the nurseries of many of our important food fishes. How well we control industrialization along our coasts, disposal of the wastes of our cities and our ships, and the dumping of nuclear wastes in the sea will determine to a great degree the future well-being of the sea's great living resources.

Mineral Resources

The ocean is the depository[15] for the world's minerals. It has been said that the waters of the sea contain about 50 quadrillion tons of dissolved mineral salts. At least 50 of the basic elements have been found in sea water, and it probably is only a matter of time until all will be found there. Minerals have been accumulating in the sea for a billion years or more. Ashes from volcanoes sifting into the rivers are carried to the sea, bringing chlorine and sulfur; undersea volcanoes supply many minerals such as boron, iodine, sulfur, and chlorine. Soil-laden waters carry calcium and silicon from weathering rock and eroding land down to the sea. Thus it is expected that the mineral wealth of the sea will continue to increase.

Our great petroleum resource also had its origin in the sea, whether along the edges of the sea where once-submerged lands have raised, as in the Middle East and in the Gulf of Mexico, or in areas once covered by ancient inland seas, as in Oklahoma. In recent years, geologists have tapped the Continental Shelves seeking oil deposits that might be held beneath the floor of the sea. As a result, offshore wells are producing oil today off the coasts of Texas and Louisiana in the Gulf of Mexico and off California.

"But why," you may ask, "are the waters of the sea salty while river waters are fresh?" The reasons for the saltiness of the sea are complicated, but a simple explanation is possible. Most rivers and other land drainage contain small quantities of dissolved salts. For billions of years this solution has been accumulating in the sea. The water, on the contrary, is removed from the sea by evaporation. It falls on the land as rain or snow and returns to the sea with more salt. The sea is so large that the concentration of dissolved salts increases very slowly indeed, too slowly for man to measure.

---

15. depository: receiving area; place where things are put or stored

---

From *Our Living Oceans,* by the U.S. Department of Commerce, National Oceanic and Atmospheric Administration

What do you think the world would be like if all life in the oceans died? The following selection first appeared as an introduction to a book about the oceans. It was written by the famous ocean explorer Jacques Cousteau. Read to find out why the author believes we must protect ocean life.

Comstock

If the Oceans Should Die

It is a shocking paradox[1] that at the precise moment in history when people are arriving at an understanding of the sea we should also have to face the question above. Just now, in our generation, when after many thousands of years of ignorance and superstitions people are at last beginning to learn about managing and exploiting the vast resources of 70 percent of earth's surface, we find ourselves in a race against time to rescue it from our own spoliations.[2]

If the oceans of earth should die—that is, if life in the oceans were suddenly, somehow to come to an end—it would be the final as well as the greatest catastrophe in the troublous story of humankind and the other animals and plants with whom we share this planet.

To begin with, bereft[3] of life the ocean would at once foul. Such a colossal stench born of decaying organic[4] matter would rise from the

---

1. paradox: surprising contradiction; puzzle
2. spoliations: acts that injure beyond repair
3. bereft: left without; lacking
4. organic: alive, once alive, or coming from a living thing

GREENHOUSE EFFECT

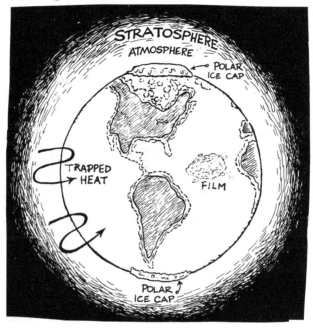

ocean wasteland that it would of itself suffice to drive people back from all coastal regions. Far harsher consequences would soon follow. The ocean is earth's principal buffer,[5] keeping balances intact between the different salts and gases of which our lives are composed and on which they depend. With no life in the seas the carbon dioxide content of the atmosphere would set forth on an inexorable[6] climb. When this CO_2 level passed a certain point the "greenhouse effect" would come into operation: heat radiating outwards from earth to space would be trapped beneath the stratosphere,[7] shooting up sea-level temperatures. At both North and South Poles the icecaps would melt. The oceans would rise perhaps 100 feet in a small number of years. All earth's major cities would be inundated.[8] To avoid drowning, one-third of the world's population would be compelled to flee to hills and mountains, hills and mountains unready to receive these people, unable to produce enough food for them. Among many other consequences of the death of the oceans, the surface would become coated with a thick film of dead organic matter, affecting the evaporation process, reducing rain, and starting global drought and famine.

---

5. buffer: anything that softens the shock or force of a blow; cushion
6. inexorable: unable to be stopped
7. stratosphere: region of the atmosphere that is about seven miles above the earth
8. inundated: flooded

Even now the disaster is only entering its terminal phase. Packed together on various highlands, starving, subject to bizarre storms and diseases, with families and societies totally disrupted, what is left of humankind begins to suffer from anoxia—lack of oxygen—caused by the extinction of plankton algae and the reduction of land vegetation. Pinned in the narrow belt between dead seas and sterile mountain slopes humankind coughs out its last moments in unutterable agony. Maybe 30 to 50 years after the ocean has died the last person on earth takes his own last breath. Organic life on the planet is reduced to bacteria and a few scavenger insects.

Why begin a work on the subject I love most in the world with this nightmare? Because the ocean can die—and because we want to make sure that it doesn't. People exist only because their home planet, earth, is the one celestial body we know of where life is at all possible. And life is possible on earth because earth is a "water planet"—water being a compound itself probably as rare in the universe as life, perhaps even synonymous[9] with life. Water is not only rare, not only infinitely precious—it is peculiar, with many oddities in its physical and chemical makeups. It is out of this unique nature of water, interacting with the dynamics of the world "water system," of which the sun and the ocean are the motors, that life originated. The ocean is life.

This is why we must change our attitudes toward the ocean. We must regard it as no longer a mystery, a menace, something so vast and invulnerable[10] that we need not concern ourselves with it, a dark and sinister abode[11] of secrets and wonders. Nor do we want to follow the methods of the first scientists who sailed and searched the seas to compile lists: lists of mammals, lists of seabirds, of jellyfish, of temperatures, of currents, of migratory patterns. Instead we want to explore the themes of the ocean's existence—how it moves and breathes, how it experiences dramas and seasons, how it nourishes its hosts of living things, how it harmonizes the physical and biological rhythms of the whole earth, what hurts it and what feeds it—not least of all, what are its stories.

I dedicate these books to water and the life which depends on water—and to the mother of waters: the Ocean.

---

9. **synonymous:** meaning the same as
10. **invulnerable:** safe from attack; not easily wounded or hurt
11. **abode:** living place

From *The Ocean World of Jacques Cousteau: Oasis in Space,* by Jacques Cousteau

Scientists wonder if icebergs may become a sign that world temperatures are rising.

An Icy Warning of a Global Warming?

When an iceberg twice the size of Rhode Island broke off from Antarctica in October 1987, it was clear that cartographers[12] would have to go back to the drawing board: the "calved" berg had ripped off a chunk of the southern continent's coast, gone except in memories and on maps was the Bay of Whales and its shoreline. What wasn't clear, though, was whether this frozen, 25-by-99-mile behemoth[13] signaled an ominous global warming.

Since the Industrial Revolution,[14] world temperatures have risen about 1°. Most researchers attribute this to carbon dioxide, which enters the atmosphere from the burning of such fossil fuels as coal and oil, traps heat, and thus creates a "greenhouse effect" that warms the planet. In the last 100 years, sea levels have risen about six inches, simply because water expands as it heats. If polar ice melted, too, that worrisome trend would become a global disaster. A further swell of two feet would flood most major ports.

Breakaway bergs: Has a balmier earth now begun to affect polar ice? In 1986 two other big bergs fell into Antarctica's Weddell Sea. In 12 years of peering at the oceans, satellites hadn't seen breakaway ice cubes of this proportion. It's too soon to blame the warming earth for all these bergs but, warns Bernhard Lettau of the National Science Foundation, "Global warming will undoubtedly have effects on the antarctic ice sheets."

---

12. **cartographers:** mapmakers
13. **behemoth:** something large and powerful
14. **Industrial Revolution:** beginning in England around 1750, the change in societies from depending mostly on agriculture (farming) to depending mostly on industry (machines and factories)

"An Icy Warning of a Global Warming?" from *Newsweek*